# A LANDMARK IN THE HISTORY OF WORLD THEATRE

Spain's history (1550-1...) ... wealth, world-shaking conquest, vast wars and heroic men. It was also the period of Spain's greatest development in the novel, poetry and drama. The authors of these plays are among the great geniuses of theatrical history. Their works—though largely neglected in the English-speaking world—are on a par with Sophocles, Shakespeare, Racine and Ibsen.

**ABOUT THE EDITOR** • Hymen Alpern, Ph.D., earned his doctorate in Spanish literature. His doctoral dissertation, which deals with a *comedia* of the Golden Age, was awarded the highest *La Prensa* Prize. He has taught Spanish and Spanish-American literature at New York University and the College of the City of New York. He studied at the Centro de Estudios Históricos in Madrid, and was one of the founders of the Instituto de las Españas and of the Pan American Student League. He served as national president of the American Association of Teachers of Spanish and Portuguese.

Dr. Alpern has authored, translated or edited numerous articles and textbooks dealing with the study of the Spanish language and literature, including *Diez Comedias del Siglo de Oro, Teatro Hispanoamericano, Cuatro Novelas Modernas de América Española, Las Aventuras de Don Quijote,* and *The Story of Calderón's La Vida Es Sueño*. He edited *El Eco,* a Spanish bi-weekly and was recently honored by the French Government with the decoration of *Officier de l'Ordre des Palmes Académiques*.

Dr. Alpern is at present principal of the Evander Childs High School in New York City.

# THE ANTA SERIES OF DISTINGUISHED PLAYS

A new series of anthologies sponsored by The American National Theatre and Academy in keeping with its aim "to extend the living theatre beyond its present limitations by bringing the best in the theatre to every state in the Union."

*Four Classic French Plays* (W654 60¢) Edited and with an Introduction by Helen A. Gaubert. Contains *The Cid, The Would-Be Gentleman, Phædra* and *Athaliah*.

*Three Distinctive Plays About Abraham Lincoln* (W655 60¢) Edited and with an Introduction by Willard Swire. Contains *Abraham Lincoln, The Last Days of Lincoln* and *Prologue to Glory*.

*Three Dramas of American Individualism* (W653 60¢) Edited and with Introductions by Joseph Mersand. Contains *Golden Boy, High Tor* and *The Magnificent Yankee*.

*Three Plays About Crime and Criminals* (W658 60¢) Edited and with Introductions by George Freedley. Contains *Arsenic and Old Lace, Kind Lady* and *Detective Story*.

*Three Plays About Doctors* (W656 60¢) Edited and with Introductions by Joseph Mersand. Contains *An Enemy of the People, Men in White* and *Yellow Jack*.

*Three Scandinavian Plays* (W657 60¢) Edited and with Introductions by Blanche Yurka. Contains *The Father, The Lady from the Sea* and *The Wild Duck*.

*Three Plays About Marriage* (W659 60¢) Edited and with Introductions by Joseph Mersand. Contains *Craig's Wife, They Knew What They Wanted* and *Holiday*.

*the* ANTA *series of distinguished plays*

# THREE CLASSIC SPANISH PLAYS

**THE SHEEP WELL**
*by Lope de Vega*

**LIFE IS A DREAM**
*by Calderón de la Barca*

**NONE BENEATH THE KING**
*by Rojas Zorrilla*

*Edited and with Introductions by
Hymen Alpern, Ph.D.*

**WASHINGTON SQUARE PRESS, INC. • NEW YORK**

# THREE CLASSIC SPANISH PLAYS

## 1963

THE SHEEP WELL by Lope de Vega is reprinted with the permission of Charles Scribner's Sons from FOUR PLAYS BY LOPE DE VEGA, translated by John Garrett Underhill. Copyright, 1936, by John Garrett Underhill.

Acknowledgement is made to the Houghton Mifflin Co. for the inclusion of LIFE IS A DREAM by Calderón de la Barca and translated by D. F. MacCarthy from THE CHIEF EUROPEAN DRAMATISTS edited by Brander Matthews.

NONE BENEATH THE KING by Rojas Zorrilla and translated by Isaac Goldberg is reprinted with the permission of Haldeman-Julius Co. Copyright, 1924 and 1951, by Haldeman-Julius Co.

*A new edition of a distinguished literary work now made available in an inexpensive, well-designed format*

L

Published by
Washington Square Press, Inc.: Executive Offices, 630 Fifth Avenue;
University Press Division, 32 Washington Place, New York, N.Y.

WASHINGTON SQUARE PRESS editions are distributed in the U.S. by Affiliated Publishers, a division of Pocket Books, Inc., 630 Fifth Avenue, New York 20, N.Y.

Introduction copyright, ©, 1963, by Washington Square Press, Inc.
*Printed in the U.S.A.*

# CONTENTS

| | |
|---|---:|
| THE GOLDEN AGE OF SPANISH LITERATURE | vii |
| INTRODUCTION | 3 |
| **The Sheep Well** <br> *by Lope de Vega* <br> *translated by John Garrett Underhill* | 11 |
| INTRODUCTION | 73 |
| **Life Is a Dream** <br> *by Calderón de la Barca* <br> *translated by Denis Florence MacCarthy* | 79 |
| INTRODUCTION | 177 |
| **None Beneath the King** <br> *by Rojas Zorrilla* <br> *translated by Isaac Goldberg* | 183 |

Any group that wishes to produce any of these plays will find production information for each play on page 230.

# The Golden Age of Spanish Literature

It is as accurate to divide time into periods as it is to carve the sea with a knife and plant straws within it to indicate boundaries. Yet man must set milestones or else he will be lost in the wilderness of his days. And if, between one milestone and another—generation or century—something strangely beautiful or admirable blossoms, he rapturously calls it "The Golden Age." It must, however, always be done as he looks backward, for as he lives in the present, the age is too replete with tribulations, cares, burdens, strife, and he is blind to genius and to greatness. Man has ever the habit of turning his back upon the sun and bending knee to candles.

The "Golden Age of Spanish Literature"—or rather, more modestly, the Golden Century (*El Siglo de Oro*)—has been set arbitrarily by scholars, as beginning in the year 1592, when Lope appeared as dramatic author, and ending with the death of Calderón in the year 1680.

Quite naturally, it was also the golden period of Spanish history. Spain still had a vast continent under heel, and the disaster of the Armada had not yet signified the end of her glory. Nor had grievous retribution for her vast injustice to Jews and Moors as yet befallen her. It was already adumbrated, to be sure, but it was not recognized, and the Iberian Peninsula seethed with life, pleasure and illusion—excellent medium for the theater.

Although the dramatic productions during the Golden Age were called *comedias*, they were not *comedies* in our modern sense, but *dramas*, even as Dante's *Divine Comedy* was not calculated for laughter with its terrifying Hell and its eternal retributive justice. The Spanish plays were of manifold varieties in three acts, and in verse. Poetry was still the Queen of Letters and not the scullery maid of our days.

Lope is generally credited with establishing the definitive norms of the national Spanish *comedia*. He set the example with plays that were realistic in background and details, were romantic in disregard of classical rules and gave freedom to the poet's phantasy.

The whole nation seemed to be play-mad. Numerous troupes of strolling players toured to the remotest villages and performed the *comedias* wherever there were groups of Spaniards, however poor or humble. To meet the public demand for *comedias* written by Lope and Calderón, the two greatest and most popular dramatists of the time, many writers did not hesitate to attribute their inferior productions to the authorship of the great masters. (This species of theft was very common for centuries throughout Europe until the advent of the copyright laws.)

While the plots are at times extremely complicated and replete with involved intrigues, sub-plots and tangential and remotely related digressions, extravagant descriptions, forced humor and bombastic declamations, the main themes revolve chiefly around the popular trilogy of *Dios, El Rey, y Mi Dama* (God, The King, and My Lady), the last named motif embodying both the sentiment of love and the duty of honor.

Among the various classifications of the *comedia* are the following common types:—

1. *Comedias heroicas* or *Comedias historiales*. These deal with heroic, historical or legendary themes. They involve kings and princes with some historical, mythological or legendary foundation. *Fuente Ovejuna* (*The Sheep Well*), is an example of this category.

2. *Comedias de capa y espada*, dramas of cloak and sword. They are plays of intrigue dealing with ordinary current life. Gallantry is their main principle, with emphasis on the *pundonor*, the exaggerated "point of honor" of the Spaniards. The principal personages belong to the genteel portion of

society dressed in cloak and sword for concealment and self-defense. *Del Rey Abajo Ninguno* (*None Beneath the King*) is *comedia de capa y espada*.

3. *Comedias palaciegas* or *comedias de palacio*, in which the action revolves around some monarch or royal personage, not strictly historical, develops in some foreign court, serving as a pretext for expounding a philosophic theory, its plot consisting of intrigue, jealousy, love and honor. The outstanding model of this type is *La Vida Es Sueño* (*Life Is a Dream*).

One of the chief virtues of the *comedias* is the generally fresh-flowing and effective versification. The variety of meters used is remarkable. The most common verse form is the *romance*, which is usually octosyllabic, and consists in the identity in the even-numbered lines of the last accented vowels. The *redondilla*, which after the *romance* is the most popular characteristic form of Spanish meter, is a quatrain of eight-syllable verses of which the first usually rhymes with the fourth, and the second with the third.

The present volume contains a significant example of each of the three main types of *comedias*. The first one, *The Sheep Well*, is an excellent dramatization of the remarkable spirit of democracy and the power of mass action in Old Spain. The second, *Life Is a Dream*, is a masterpiece of the philosophical drama, a genre in which Spaniards do not ordinarily excel. The third, *None Beneath the King*, deals with the aforementioned *pundonor*, a popular dramatic motive that exalts the extreme sensitivity of Spanish honor, a trait of the national character of Spain for many centuries, not only during the *Siglo de Oro*.

In addition to the three *comedias* in the present volume, other well-known *comedias* of the *Siglo de Oro*, most of which unfortunately are not available in English translation, are the following:—

*Las Mocedades del Cid* (*Youthful Adventures of the Cid*) by Guillén de Castro, the first dramatization of the Cid legend, and the inspiration for Corneille's *Le Cid*, the first great French tragedy.

*El Burlador de Sevilla* (*Love Rogue*) by Tirso de Moli[na] the first dramatization of the Don Juan legend.

*La Verdad Sospechosa* (*The Doubtful Man*) by Ruiz [de] Alarcón, the greatest Spanish work of dramatic moralizati[on] and the basis for the first important French comedy, Corneil[le's] *Le Menteur*.

*La Estrella de Sevilla* (*The Star of Seville*), of uncerta[in] authorship, although attributed to Lope, a marvellously co[n]structed and technically perfect example of the "capa [y] espada" genre.

*El Desdén con el Desdén* (*Disdain Met with Disdain*) [by] Moreto, an excellent "comedia de carácter."

*El Esclavo del Demonio* (*Slave of the Devil*) by Mira [de] Amescua, a noted religious play resembling the Faust legen[d.]

In a generation so intent upon disturbing the peace of t[he] moon and hurling rockets to dance around the sun, it wou[ld] be well to plant once more our feet upon the good Mother, t[he] Earth, who welcomes the burden, and upon whose face m[en] have created things of beauty and of truth. For how shall [we] understand the present, if we disdain the past? How know t[he] child and ignore his parents and his parents' parents? Eve[ry] generation is a link in the great chain of time, and letting o[ne] rust, we imperil the whole.

Now, with our Prologue ended, let the curtain rise!

HYMEN ALPERN

# THE SHEEP WELL

# Lope de Vega

Félix Lope de Vega (1562-1635), Spain's most brilliant dramatist of the Golden Age, was called *Un Monstruo de la Naturaleza* (A prodigy of nature) by his contemporary, the great Cervantes. Others referred to him at the time as *Fénix de los Ingenios* (Phoenix, or King, of the talented). Almost without exception, contemporary playwrights acknowledged his supremacy, and literary critics since his time have revered him not only as a great creative genius but also as the creator of a national drama. Lope was certainly one of the most striking personalities of the most colorful period in Spanish history, the age of Cervantes, Velásquez, El Greco.

Born in northwestern Spain on the ancestral estate of Vega two years before Shakespeare, Lope was an extraordinarily precocious child, writing verse when very young and authoring a full-length play of merit at the age of fourteen. He attended the University of Alcalá, then enlisted as a soldier and took part in the unfortunate expedition of the Invincible Armada. While others were shedding their blood, he is said to have spent most of his time below decks writing eleven thousand verses of an epic poem. Thereafter, he led a very active life, not devoted exclusively to literary work. It was a life of inglorious contradictions. He took religious orders, partly because he found church life a means of securing leisure. He was at the same time priest and libertine, and spent most of his non-writing time going from sin to repentance, and from repentance back to sin—a volcano of passion and creation. Only as we accept the miracle of genius can we relate, without explaining, this prodigy of nature who left behind him so vast a monument of magnificent work and so long and luminous a caravan of ladies worshipping at his altar. Alas, poor Don Juan!

What was he by comparison but an amateur; and Solomon th{e} Magnificent had a thousand wives, but how many sweethearts{?}

Despite his very self-indulgent, immoral life—or perhap{s} because of it—Lope wrote some of the best devout poems i{n} Spanish. Often saints begin life as sinners, and Francis of Assis{i} could not have blossomed into the Flower of Virtue withou{t} having been first pricked by the thorn of vice. While it wa{s} common knowledge that there was little in Lope's character t{o} admire, he was so loved and honored that his funeral laste{d} nine whole days. Doubtless, mingled with lamentation ther{e} was also celebration, for man is a tragi-comedian, mixin{g} sorrow with pleasure.

Lope was a writer of prodigious fecundity. He was th{e} author of some one thousand eight hundred plays (not to men{-}tion his incredible productivity in every other form of literatur{e} current in his day)—a total of over twenty-two million lines{.} His biographer, Montalván, alleged that he wrote five ful{l} length *comedias* at Toledo in fifteen days. Lope himself ad{-}mitted that he averaged one hundred *comedias* a year after ag{e} fifty, adding that "more than a hundred of my *comedias* hav{e} taken only twenty-four hours to pass from my brain to th{e} boards of the theatre." Too great a burden to carry across th{e} desert of time, and many a camel perished with its cargo!

His most notable plays are those inspired by national his{-}tory, and his lasting contribution is the *capa y espada* (cloa{k} and sword) drama. His theatre, because of his fertility in in{-}venting plots, his mastery of dialogue, and his inventions i{n} form and language, became the classic theatre of Spain. H{e} did not write plays to be read but to be acted, for he wa{s} interested in pleasing the multitude. *Fuente Ovejuna* is jus{t} such a play—a historical drama designed especially to appea{l} to the masses.

Lope's chief characteristics as a dramatic writer are variet{y} and fertility; subordination of all interests to the interest o{f} the story; intriguing plots and comic underplots. His is {a} theatre of action, not of reflection, description or characte{r} delineation. Lope is not profound, but clear and graceful. H{e} is vigorous rather than finished. His chief faults are loosenes{s} nd want of polish. He generally lacks universal appeal, but is influence on other Spanish dramatists was profound. Through him, the entire Spanish classical theatre became unique, genuinely national, and unaffected by foreign influence.

For him whose appetite has been whetted there is good material for further study:

(1) a scholarly biography by H. A. Rennert, *The Life of Lope de Vega*, Philadelphia, 1904.
(2) a critical analysis of the magnitude of Lope's labors by R. Schevill, *The Dramatic Art of Lope de Vega*, Berkeley, 1918.
(3) a fictionalized biography by Angel Flores, *Lope de Vega: Master of Nature*. New York, 1926.

# The Sheep Well
(*Fuente Ovejuna*)

This is one of Lope's magnificent plays which was popular in Spain of the seventeenth century and is gaining in popularity in the twentieth century throughout the world. Translations are now available in English, French, German and Russian. It has been produced within recent years in various European lands and is probably enjoying a following in the emerging African and Asiatic countries. It was popular in Czarist Russia and has been staged as a ballet in the Soviet Union and also on the movie screen in Mexico.

The reason for the great and lasting popularity of this play is its excellent dramatization of the remarkable spirit of democracy and the power of mass action. Its theme is the uprising of an entire village against the abuses of an overlord. Its hero is not one individual, but the entire village. Writing of the people with sympathetic understanding, Lope portrays with powerful strokes the qualities of the Spanish peasant—valor, heroism, courtesy, integrity, honor, as well as respect for the sanctity of personal dignity and individual liberty. He recognizes the existence of honor in the common man in whose veins courses only red blood—Nature's vulgar fluid! These qualities as well as collective vengeance and the rugged vindication of democracy are developed with refreshing simplicity coupled with imposing power and grandeur.

The play, based on a true historical event, owes its title to a little town of the same name where the principal action takes place. In 1476, during the reign of the Catholic monarchs, the honest, law-abiding villagers of Fuente Ovejuna, goaded to fury by the intolerable oppression and brazen excesses of their

*Comendador* (Overlord), who governed in a tyrannical manner and seduced or abducted their wives and daughters, rose in revolt, attacked his castle and killed him. The King and Queen (Ferdinand and Isabella) ordered an investigation of the killing, but the village took collective responsibility for the act, refusing in the face of threats and torture to reveal whose hand had struck the blow. When the royal investigator questioned the defendants, each one—young and old alike—in turn gave the same reply, thus:

"Who killed the Comendador?"

"Fuente Ovejuna, Sir."

"And who is Fuente Ovejuna?"

"We all are one."

The Sovereigns, disarmed by the heroism of the people and noted for their administration of justice wherever it was a matter of a struggle of the Third Estate against the turbulent feudal lords, terminated the case by issuing a full pardon to the revolutionary village and attaching it directly to the crown. And so justice and profit went hand in hand, as it generally happens when the mighty deal with the humble.

Thus, *Fuente Ovejuna* is a drama which, without impairment of the monarchical sentiment peculiar to the period, legitimizes rebellion against despotism. It is for this reason that certain social restlessness and political tendencies of our time have come to give the play renewed interest. Lope's extraordinary and powerful portrayal of mob psychology presages its permanent popularity. However, it is not only the chief plot—the nobles vs. the people—but the minor interwoven sub-plots, revealing with faultless logic and power the every-day life and customs and soul of the Spanish peasants, which assures *Fuente Ovejuna* a permanent place in the world's repertory of theatrical masterpieces.

# THE SHEEP WELL

# Characters

THE KING, FERDINAND OF ARAGON
QUEEN ISABELLA OF CASTILE
DON MANRIQUE, MASTER OF SANTIAGO
RODRIGO TÉLLEZ GIRÓN, GRAND MASTER OF CALATRAVA
THE COMMANDER FERNÁN GÓMEZ DE GUZMÁN
FLORES  
ORTUÑO } *his retainers*
CIMBRANOS, *a soldier*
A JUDGE
TWO REGIDORS OF CIUDAD REAL
ESTEBAN  
ALONSO } *Alcaldes of Fuente Ovejuna*
JUAN ROJO  
CUADRADO } *Regidors*
ANOTHER REGIDOR of *Fuente Ovejuna*
FRONDOSO  
MENGO } *peasants*
BARRILDO
LEONELO, *a student*
A FARMER
A SOLDIER
LAURENCIA  
PASCUALA } *peasant girls*
JACINTA
A BOY

MUSICIANS, SOLDIERS, FARMERS, VILLAGERS
AND ATTENDANTS

*The scene is laid in Almagro, the village of Fuente Ovejuna, the country round about Ciudad Real, and at the itinerant Royal Court in Castile*
*Time: 1476*

# ACT I

(*A Street in Almagro.*)

(*The* COMMANDER *enters with* FLORES *and* ORTUÑO, *servants.*)

COMMANDER: Does the Master know I have come to town?
FLORES: He does, sir.
ORTUÑO: The years will bring discretion.
COMMANDER: I am Fernán Gómez de Guzmán.
FLORES: To-day youth may serve as his excuse.
COMMANDER: If he is ignorant of my name, let him respect the dignity of the High Commander.
ORTUÑO: He were ill advised to fail in courtesy.
COMMANDER: Or he will gain little love. Courtesy is the key to favor while discourtesy is stupidity that breeds enmity.
ORTUÑO: Should a rude oaf hear how roundly he was hated, with the whole world at his heels not to bark but to bite, he would die sooner than convict himself a boor.
FLORES: Slight no man. Among equals pride is folly but toward inferiors it becomes oppression. Here neglect is want of care. The boy has not yet learned the price of favor.
COMMANDER: The obligation which he assumed with the sword the day that the cross of Calatrava was fixed upon his breast, bound him to humility and love.
FLORES: He can intend no contempt that his quick spirit shall not presently make appear.
ORTUÑO: Return, sir, nor stay upon his pleasure.
COMMANDER: I have come to know this boy.
(*Enter the* MASTER OF CALATRAVA *and* ATTENDANTS)
MASTER: A thousand pardons, Fernán Gómez de Guzmán! I am advised of your arrival in the city.

COMMANDER: I had just complaint of you, for my affection and our birth are holy ties, being as we are the one Master of Calatrava, and the other Commander, who subscribes himself yours wholly.

MASTER: I had no thought of this purposed honor, Fernando, hence a tardy welcome. Let me embrace you once again.

COMMANDER: Vying in honor. I have staked my own on your behalf in countless causes, even answering during your minority before the Pope at Rome.

MASTER: You have indeed. By the holy token that we bear above our hearts, I repay your love, and honor you as I should my father.

COMMANDER: I am well content.

MASTER: What news of the war at the front?

COMMANDER: Attend and learn your obligation.

MASTER: Say I am already in the field.

COMMANDER: Noble Master
Don Rodrigo Téllez Girón,
To power and rule exalted
Through bravery of a mighty sire
Who eight years since
Renounced the Mastership,
Devising it to you,
As was confirmed by oaths and surety
Of Kings and High Commanders,
Even the Sovereign Pontiff,
Pius the Second,
Concurring by his bull,
And later Paul, succeeding him,
Decreeing holily
That Don Juan Pacheco,
Noble Master of Santiago,
Should co-adjutor be
With you to serve,
Till now, his death recorded,
All government and rule
Descend upon your head,
Sole and supreme

# The Sheep Well

Despite your untried years.
Wherefore take counsel,
Harkening to the voice of honor,
And follow the commitment
Of kin and allies, wisely led.
Henry the Fourth is dead.
Let all his lieges
Bend the knee forthwith
To Alonso, King of Portugal,
Heir by right in Castile
Through his wife
In tie of marriage,
Though Ferdinand,
Lord of Aragon,
Like right maintains
By title of his wife,
Isabella.
Yet to our eyes
The line of her succession is not clear,
Nor can we credit
Shadow of deception
In the right descent
Of Juana, now secure
Under the protection of your cousin,
Who loves you as a brother.
Therefore summon all the Knights
Of Calatrava to Almagro,
Thence to reduce
Ciudad Real,
Which guards the pass
Dividing Andalusia from Castile,
On both
Frowning impartially.
Few men will gain the day.
For want of soldiers
The people mount the walls,
Aided by errant knights
Faithful to Isabella,

And so pledged to Ferdinand
As King.
Strike terror, Rodrigo,
To the hearts of those who say
That this great cross
Rests heavily
Upon the sagging bosom of a child.
Consider the Counts of Ureña,
From whom you spring,
Flaunting the laurels of their might
Upon the heights of fame,
Nor neglect to emulate
The Marquises of Villena,
With other gallant captains
Whose names in manifold
Brighten the outstretched wings
Of reputation.
Unsheathe your virgin sword
Till in battle, like the cross,
It drip with blood.
Of this red cross,
Blasoned on the breast,
Breathes there no votary
Whose drawn sword flashes white.
At the breast the one,
At the side the other
Must glow and flame with red!
So crown, valiant Girón,
With deeds
The immortal temple
Reared stone by stone
By your great ancestors.

MASTER: Fernán Gómez,
I shall march with you
Because our cause is just,
And with my kin bear arms.
If I must pass,
Then shall I pass at Ciudad Real

As a lightning stroke,
Cleaving as I pass,
While my scant years proclaim
To friend and foe alike
That when my uncle died
Was no mortality of valor.
I draw my sword
That men may see it shine,
Livid with the passion of the cross,
Maculately red.
Where hold you residence?
Send on your vassals
To combat in my train.

COMMANDER: Few but faithful serve,
Who will contend like lions
In battle.
Fuente Ovejuna is a town
Of simple folk,
Unskilled in warfare,
Rather with plough and spade
Tilling the fields.

MASTER: Fuente Ovejuna, glebe of peace!

COMMANDER: Favored possession
In these troubled times,
Pastoral, serene!
Gather your men;
Let none remain unarmed.

MASTER: To-day I spur my horse
And level my eager lance.


(*The Square of Fuente Ovejuna*)

(PASCUALA *and* LAURENCIA *enter*)

LAURENCIA: I prayed he would never come back.
PASCUALA: When I brought the word I knew it would grieve you.

LAURENCIA: Would to God he had never seen Fuente Ovejuna.

PASCUALA: Laurencia, many a girl has made a pretense of saying no, yet all the while her heart has been as soft as butter in her.

LAURENCIA: I am a live-oak, gnarled and twisted.

PASCUALA: Yes, but why refuse a drink of water?

LAURENCIA: I do, be the sun never so hot, though you may not believe it. Why love Fernando? He's no husband.

PASCUALA: No, woman.

LAURENCIA: And amen! Plenty of girls in the village have trusted the Commander to their harm.

PASCUALA: It will be a miracle if you escape.

LAURENCIA: You are blind, because I have avoided him a full month now, Pascuala, and no quarter. Flores, who lays his snares, and that villain Ortuño, offered me a waist, necklace and a head-dress. They praised Fernando, the master, and pictured him so great that I blushed at his very glory, but for all that they could not move me.

PASCUALA: But where was this?

LAURENCIA: Down by the brook there, a week gone yesterday.

PASCUALA: You're already lost, Laurencia.

LAURENCIA: No, no, no!

PASCUALA: Maybe the priest might believe your story.

LAURENCIA: I am too innocent for the priest. In His Name, Pascuala, but of a morning rising early I had rather set me a slice of ham on the fire to munch with a crust of bread of my own kneading, filching a glass meanwhile out of the old stopped butt, once mother's back is turned, to wet my thirst, and then climb up to watch the cow thrash through the cabbages, all foaming at the mouth come noon-day, while I hearten myself with a bit of eggplant and a strip of bacon after hard walking, and return weary toward supper-time to nibble the raisins, home-grown in our own vineyard, which God fend the hail from, sitting me down with a dish of salad and pepper and olive oil, and so to bed tired at nightfall, in contentment and peace, with prayer on my lips to be preserved from the men, devils, God knows, every one, than I would deliver myself up to their

## The Sheep Well

wiles for all their love and fury. What they want is to undo us, joy in the night and at dawning a maid's mourning.

PASCUALA: You are right, Laurencia, for a sated lover flies faster than a farm sparrow. In the winter when the fields are bare they sing 'tweet' under the eaves till they come by the crumbs from the farmer's board, but when the fields are green and frost has been forgotten, instead of fluttering down to sing 'tweet' they hop up to the roof-tree and cry 'twit,' and 'twit' it is at you standing down below, make the most that you can of their twitting. Men are the same. When they need us we are their very lives, their heart, their soul, their entire being, but their hunger satisfied off they fly and leave us, too, with the echo of their twitting. So I say no man can be trusted.

(MENGO, BARRILDO and FRONDOSO *enter*)

FRONDOSO: You defeat yourself, Barrildo.

BARRILDO: Two judges are here who can decide between us.

MENGO: Agree upon the forfeit and then we'll call in the girls. If they favor me, you hand me both your shirts, with whatever else you have on your backs, in meed of victory.

BARRILDO: Agreed. But what will you give if you lose?

MENGO: My rebeck of old box, which is worth more than a granary, for God knows its like cannot be bought in the village.

BARRILDO: Fairly said and offered.

FRONDOSO: Done!—God save you, ladies.

LAURENCIA: Frondoso calls us ladies.

FRONDOSO: The flattery of the age.
  The blind we say are one-eyed,
  The cross-eyed merely squint,
  Pupils equal masters
  While cripples barely limp;
  The spendthrift fools call "open,"
  The dumb now hold their tongues,
  Bullies out-vie brave men,
  Shouters shame the grave men,
  And as for saving
  Praise the miser—

None so active as the meddler
To promote the common good.
Gossips will "talk freely,"
While concede we must
The quarrelsome are just.
Boasters display their courage,
The shrinking coward "retires,"
The impudent grow witty,
The taciturn sit pretty,
All hail the idiot.
Gamblers, pray, "look forward,"
The bald deserve respect,
Admit the ass is graceful,
That large feet proclaim the faithful,
While a blotched and pimpled face-full
Is a scientific indication
Of a sluggish circulation.
The lie to-day a truth is,
Rudeness clever youth is,
And if you have a hump,
Why follow your bent
All the way over,
Without stooping
Moreover,
And so to conclude
I call you ladies,

For otherwise there is no telling what names I might ca you.

LAURENCIA: In the city praise may be the fashion, Frondos but by my faith we have a contrary custom in the countr where words are sharp and barbed, upon tongues that a calloused to use them.

FRONDOSO: Who speaks knows.

LAURENCIA: Turn all in reverse.
Know and be a bore,
Work and you have luck,
The prudent are faint-hearted,
The upright reek with muck.

# The Sheep Well

>                Advice to-day spells insult,
>                Charity rank waste,
>                Be fair and painted ugly,
>                Be good, what wretched taste!
>                Truth is made for boobies,
>                No purity wins rubies,
>                While as for giving,
>                'Tis a veil for sinful living,
>                Fie, fie the hypocrite!
>                Disparage true worth always.
>                Dub simple faith imbecility,
>                Flat cowardice amiability,
>                Nor ever be fearful
>                Against the innocent
>                To speak an ear-full.
>                No woman is honest,
>                No beauty is chaste,
>                And as for virtue
>                There is not enough to hurt you,
>                For in the country
>                A curse
>                Turns merit to reverse.

MENGO: Devil of a girl!

BARRILDO: On my soul, she is too quick for us!

MENGO: A pinch of spice plashed into the holy water the day of her christening.

AURENCIA: Well, well, since you question us, let us have it without delay and judge truly.

FRONDOSO: I'll set out the argument.

LAURENCIA: Plant in season, then, and begin.

FRONDOSO: Attend, Laurencia.

LAURENCIA: Oh, I'll have an answer for you some day.

FRONDOSO: Be fair, be just.

LAURENCIA: What is this wager?

FRONDOSO: Barrildo and I oppose Mengo.

LAURENCIA: Mengo is right. So, there!

BARRILDO: A fact is certain and plain which he denies.

MENGO: I deny it because it's a lie and they wander from t[he] mark.

LAURENCIA: Explain.

BARRILDO: He maintains there is no such thing as love.

LAURENCIA: Then it takes hold of one mightily.

BARRILDO: Yes, though it be blind, for without love the wor[ld] would never go on.

MENGO: I say little, not being able to read, though I cou[ld] learn, but if the elements make the world and our bodies a[re] made of the elements which war against each other u[n]ceasingly, causing anger and discord, then where is lov[e?]

BARRILDO: Mengo, the world is love, here and hereafter, n[o] discord. Harmony is love. Love is a reaching out.

MENGO: A pulling in, according to nature, which governs a[ll] things through the resemblances that are. Love is a looki[ng] to its own, it's preservation. I raise my hand to my face [to] prevent the blow, I move my feet to remove me from dang[er] to my body, my eye-lids close to shield my sight throug[h] the attraction of a mutual love.

PASCUALA: He admits it's love, so what then? There's an en[d.]

MENGO: We love ourselves, no one else, that's flat.

PASCUALA: Mengo, what a lie! And God forgive me. The lo[ve] a man bears for a woman, or a beast for its mate, is a fierc[e] consuming passion.

MENGO: Self-love, interest, not pure love. What is love?

LAURENCIA: A running after beauty.

MENGO: But why run after beauty?

LAURENCIA: For the thrill and the pleasure, boy.

MENGO: True. And the pleasure a man seeks for himself.

LAURENCIA: True again.

MENGO: So that self-love seeks its own delight?

LAURENCIA: Granted.

MENGO: Therefore there is no love, only we like what we lik[e] and we intend in all things to get it, to seek delight, o[ur] delight.

BARRILDO: One day the priest preached in the village about [a] man named Plato who had taught men how to love, b[ut]

# The Sheep Well

what Plato loved, he said, was the soul and the virtue that was hidden in it.

PASCUALA: So the fathers teach the children in 'cademies and schools.

LAURENCIA: Yes, and don't you listen to any nonsense, either. Mengo, thank God you never knew the curse of love.

MENGO: Were you ever in love?

LAURENCIA: In love with my honor, always.

FRONDOSO: Come, come, ladies! Decide, decide.

BARRILDO: Who wins?

PASCUALA: Let the priest or the sacristan cook up a reply, for Laurencia loves too much and I not a little, so how can we, siding both ways, decide?

FRONDOSO: They laugh at us.

(*Enter* FLORES)

FLORES: God guard the fair!

PASCUALA: This man is from the Commander.

LAURENCIA: Why so brash, old goshawk, in the village?

FLORES: You meet me as a soldier.

LAURENCIA: From Don Fernando?

FLORES: The war is done, though it has cost us blood, and armies of our friends.

FRONDOSO: Say what of note our band achieved.

FLORES: I will, and that better than another, having seen it with my own eyes.

Beleaguering the city
Of Ciudad Real,
By charter royal,
The valiant Master mustered in
Two thousand foot,
Bravest among his vassals,
Beside three hundred horse,
Churchmen and laymen,
For the crimson cross
Summons to its aid
Those who profess it on their breasts
Though robed and habited for prayer,

Crusading oft in holy cause,
Ruthless to slay the Moor.
Boldly the lad rode forth,
His tunic green
Embroidered with golden scrolls,
While silken cords
Caught up his sleeves,
Stayed sixfold
Above his iron gauntlets.
His steed was sturdy stout,
A dappled roan
Bred beside the Betis,
Drinking of the willing stream
And pasturing on lush meadows,
But now in panoply of white
Bedecked, patterns of net
Flecking the snowy pools
That gemmed his mottled hide
From plumèd crest
Down to the buckskin tail-piece.
At equal pace
The Commander Fernán Gómez
Bestrid a piebald charger,
Black of mane, the tail coal black,
White foaming at the nostril.
A Turkish coat of mail he wore,
Breastplate and corselet
Glowing bright orange,
Relieved with pearls and gold.
White plumes
Topped off his helmet,
Pallid plumes wind-blown,
Striking dismay,
The while his puissant arm
Banded now red, now white,
Brandished an ash-tree,
Famous as his lance

Even to Granada.
The city flew to arms,
Vain boasts of loyalty
With greed contending,
Some fearful for their homes,
Some of their treasure.
The Master breached those walls,
Flung back those surly churls,
And the heads
Of the rebel leaders,
As of those conspiring there
Against his dignity,
With a blow
Severed from the body.
We gagged the common folk,
Then beat them openly,
So in that town
The Master is feared and praised
Conjointly.
Though few in years,
By deeds, by valor and by victory
Nature in him has forged
A bolt from heaven
To rive Africa,
Her blue moon senescent
To the red cross bowed,
Obeisant.
Rich the promise
Of the rape of this fair city,
With apportionment
Of present gain
To him and the Commander.
Now hear the music sound, for zest in victory adds sweetest savor.

(*The* COMMANDER *enters with* ORTUÑO *and* MUSICIANS, *accompanied by* JUAN ROJO, *Regidor*, ESTEBAN *and* ALONSO, *Alcaldes*)

### Song

*Welcome, great Commander,*
*Many times a victor,*
*Men and fields mowed down!*
*Guzmáns, arm, to battle!*
*Girones, strike, to battle!*
*Doves in peace,*
*Mighty in repose.*
*Forward to the conflict,*
*Strong of limb as oak-trees,*
*Drive the Moors before you*
*From Ciudad Real.*
*Flaunt your pennons proudly*
*In Fuente Ovejuna,*
*Valiant Fernán Gómez,*
*Glorious Conqueror!*

COMMANDER: Acknowledgment and thanks in this our town
 Receive in token of the love you show.
ALONSO: Accept this rustic tribute to renown,
 Proffered how simply. These poor meadows grow
Scant sustenance of woe.
ESTEBAN:                              Welcome acce[pt]
 To Fuente Ovejuna, whose elders glow
 With pride, offering homely gifts, yet apt
To please, as pod or sprout or root, in carts
Heaped high with ruddy fruits, the produce rept
 From field and orchard, ripening in our hearts,
Mellowed in crib and barnyard. First, car one
Twin hampers bears of jars, baked for these marts,
 Whereto are added geese that sleekly run
Long necks from tangling nets, and shrilly shriek
Cackles of praise, pæans of booty won.
 Ten salted hogs bid the next wagon creak,
Bulging with fatty trimmings and dried meat;
The skins like amber shine, side, haunch and breek.
 A hundred pair of capon follow, treat

For the belly, plump hens torn from the cock
Through all the eager farms, tender and meet
   For axing. Arms we lack, nor bring we stock
Of blooded steeds, nor harness for the bold,
For such in rustic hands were cheat and mock
   Of love's pure gold which in our hearts is told.
Twelve wine-skins next appear, with beady wine
Filled full, in winter enemy of cold
   And friendly to the soldier, ally in line
Of battle, or on defense trusty like steel,
Tempering courage, for temper springs of wine.
   Unnumbered cheeses, last, jounce past awheel,
With products of the churn and dairy days,
True tokens of the love the people feel
Toward you and yours, harvests of heart-felt praise.

COMMANDER: Thanks and be gone, Alcaldes of this town. Be gone assured of favor.

ALONSO: Rest, Master, in enjoyment of our love. These cat-tails before the door and this coarse sedge grass should bear pearls to match your deserving, as indeed we pray, and yet fall short of the devotion of the village.

COMMANDER: I accept the gifts right gladly. So get you gone.

ESTEBAN: The singers will repeat the refrain.

### Song

*Welcome, great Commander,*
*Many times a victor,*
*Men and fields mowed down!*
(Exeunt)

COMMANDER: The girls stay behind.

LAURENCIA: No, Your Excellency.

COMMANDER: By the Lord you do! No airs nor graces! These are soldiers here.

LAURENCIA: Pascuala, he looks your way.

PASCUALA: Do you teach me to be modest?

COMMANDER: I look your way, little chuck with the crook,

and tend to this burr of the pasture, till she open to r
PASCUALA: We grew here, Master.
COMMANDER: Pass into the house where my men will ke
  you safe.
LAURENCIA: If the Alcaldes go in so will we, because one
  my father, but a girl by herself is just a girl and must
  careful.
COMMANDER: A word, Flores.
FLORES: Master?
COMMANDER: How? What mean these green-briers?
FLORES: Walk straight in, girls. Come!
LAURENCIA: You let go!
FLORES: Any fool can walk.
PASCUALA: You'll lock the door if we do go in.
FLORES: Pass and taste the spoils of war. Come!
COMMANDER: (*Aside to* ORTUÑO) Throw the bolt, Ortuí
  once they're inside.
  (*Exit*)
LAURENCIA: You hurt us, Flores.
ORTUÑO: These cheeses came in no cart.
PASCUALA: No, and we are not for you, either, so get out!
FLORES: What can you do with a girl?
LAURENCIA: Your master has his fill to-day for one stomac
ORTUÑO: He's a judge of meat and prefers you, though t
  carts pass.
LAURENCIA: Then let him burst!
  (*The girls go out*)
FLORES: What will the Master say with never a sight of
  woman for good cheer? They laugh at us.
ORTUÑO: Blows reward service, mostly given for villainy,
  there's no cure. It's dessert.


(*A tent prepared for audience*)

(*Enter the* KING DON FERDINAND OF ARAGON
*and* QUEEN ISABELLA *accompanied by* DON
MANRIQUE *and* ATTENDANTS)

## The Sheep Well

**ISABELLA:** To prepare is wise. Sire, harry Alonso of Portugal
where he has pitched his tents, for a ready offense averts
the threatened injury.

**THE KING:** Navarre and Aragon despatch swift aid and succor.
Under my command the Castilian bands shall be reformed.
Success lies in prevention.

**ISABELLA:** Majesty, prevail by strategy.

**DON MANRIQUE:** Two Regidors of Ciudad Real crave audience.

**THE KING:** Admit them to our presence.

(*Enter* Two REGIDORS *of Ciudad Real*)

**FIRST REGIDOR:** Great Ferdinand the Catholic our King,
Posting from Aragon to high Castile
On warlike service and the common weal,
Humble petition to thy sword we bring
For vengeance, urging here the patent royal
Bestowed on Ciudad Real, thy city,
Foully wronged. To be thy city was our joy,
Thy will our law, proclaimed in kingly charter;
But blows of fate laid low our fealty.
A froward youth, Rodrigo Téllez Girón,
Master of Calatrava, with naked sword
Carves out addition to his wide domain,
Wasting our homes, our lands and revenues.
We met his treacherous assault, and force
Opposed to force, by threat and fear undaunted
Till blood in rivers ran adown our streets,
Alas but vainly! The day we lost, and he,
Pricked on by the Commander Fernán Gómez,
Cunning in council, governs the city,
While we, enslaved, lament our injuries.

**THE KING:** Where dwells this Fernán Gómez?

**FIRST REGIDOR:** Sire, Fuente Ovejuna is his seat,
Wherein he rules amid his seignories.
He governs there, there does he his will,
Raining down blows upon his abject thralls
Beyond endurance.

**THE KING:** Name your captain.

SECOND REGIDOR:                              Sire,
   None lives. Not one, alas, of noble blood
   Survives unwounded, untaken or unslain.
ISABELLA: This cause demands an instant remedy.
   The walls may be surrendered to the foe,
   Who thus will boldly dominate the pass,
   Entering Extremadura from the side
   Of Portugal.
THE KING:         Set forth at once, Manrique,
   And with two chosen companies chastise
   This arrogance, denying let or stay.
   The Count of Cabra shall by our command
   As swiftly follow, bravest of the house
   Of Córdoba.
   The front of tyranny must bow
   And pride lie low
   In the presence of our majesty.
ISABELLA: Depart ambassador of victory.
   (*Exeunt*)


(*A river bank near Fuente Ovejuna. Trees and bushes*)

(LAURENCIA *and* FRONDOSO *enter*)

LAURENCIA: I had not wrung the sheets, you saucy Frondos[o] when you drove me from the river bank with spying. Wh[ile] we gaze the country-side talks and waits on tip-toe. T[he] sturdiest of our lads, your jacket is the gayest and t[he] costliest, so others note what you do, and not a girl in t[he] village nor herdsman on the hills nor down in the riv[er] bottoms but swears we are one and of right ought to [be] joined, while Juan Chamorro, the sacristan, leaves his pi[p]ing to publish the banns, for love, they say, goes first [to] church. Ah, wine burst the vaults in August, and bur[st] every pot with must but I heed them not nor attend to the[m]

# The Sheep Well

chatter, though it be time, methinks, and time soon for our own good to put an end to all this idle talk and pother.

FRONDOSO: Laughing Laurencia, I die while you smile. Though I say nothing you will not hear me, till at last I have scarcely strength even to mutter. I would be your husband but you repay with taunts my faith and loyalty.

LAURENCIA: I encourage you all I can.

FRONDOSO: It's not enough. When I think of you I cannot eat, drink or sleep. I starve yet love an angel. God knows I die.

LAURENCIA: Cross yourself, Frondoso, or else bethink you of some charm.

FRONDOSO: There's a charm for two doves at the church, love, that makes them one. God set us beak to beak!

LAURENCIA: Speak to your master, Juan Rojo, if you will, and can summon the courage, else I must, since he is my uncle. Pray for the day, and hope.

FRONDOSO: Look! The Commander!

LAURENCIA: Stalking deer. Hide in the bushes.

FRONDOSO: Big bucks are hard to hide.

(*The* COMMANDER *enters*)

COMMANDER: Aha! Following the fawn, I hit upon the doe.

LAURENCIA: I was resting from washing and return to the brookside now, Commander.

COMMANDER: Sweet Laurencia, stay, nor obscure the beauty heaven has granted to my sight. If you have escaped my hand till now, the woods and the fields will befriend us, for they are accomplices of love. Bend your pride and let your cheek flush as it has never done yet in the village. Sebastiana, who was Pedro Redondo's wife, has been mine, and so has the chit who wedded Martín del Pozo. I came upon her two nights a bride, and she opened to me fondly.

LAURENCIA: My Lord, they had opened to so many that their fondness was no longer in question. Ask the village. God grant you luck with the deer. The cross on your breast proclaims you are no tempter of women.

COMMANDER: You protest too much, lass. I put down my cross-bow. With my hands I will subdue these pretty wiles.

LAURENCIA: No, no! What would you? Let go!
   (FRONDOSO *re-enters and seizes the cross-bow*)
COMMANDER: Struggle is useless.
FRONDOSO: (*Aside*) I take the bow. Heaven grant I do n[ot]
   shoot.
COMMANDER: Yield! Have done!
LAURENCIA: Heaven help me now!
COMMANDER: We are alone, no one will hear——
FRONDOSO: Noble Commander, loose that girl, or your brea[st]
   shall be my mark, though the cross shine clear upon it.
COMMANDER: The dog insults me!
FRONDOSO: Here is no dog. Laurencia, flee!
LAURENCIA: Frondoso, you take care.
FRONDOSO: Go!
   (LAURENCIA *goes*)
COMMANDER: Only a fool deprives himself of his swor[d,]
   which I, god or devil, put by, fearing to fright the chase!
FRONDOSO: By God above, Commander, if I loose this strin[g]
   I'll gyve you like a hawk!
COMMANDER: Betrayed! Traitorous hind, deliver up that cros[s-]
   bow. Dog, set down!
FRONDOSO: To be shot through? Hardly. Love is a warrio[r]
   that yields his throne to none.
COMMANDER: Shall a knight valiant in battle be foiled by [a]
   dumb peasant? Stay, wretch! On guard!—for I forget m[y]
   rank and station.
FRONDOSO: I do not. I am a swain, but since I will to live,
   take the cross-bow with me.
COMMANDER: Ignominy, shame! I will have vengeance to th[e]
   hilt. Quickly I vanish.

# ACT II

(*Square in Fuente Ovejuna.*)

(ESTEBAN *enters with a* REGIDOR)

ESTEBAN: Better touch the reserve no further. The year bodes ill with threat of foul weather, so let the grain be impounded though there be mutiny among the people.

REGIDOR: I am of your mind if the village may be governed in peace.

ESTEBAN: Then speak to Fernán Gómez. These astrologers with their harangues pretend they know secrets God only knows. Not a scrap can they read of the future, unholy fabricators of what was and what shall be, when to their eyes even the present is blank,
> For their ignorance is rank.

Can they bring the clouds indoors and lay the stars upon the table? How do they peer into heaven and yet come down with such dire disasters? These fellows tell us how and when to sow, here with the grain, there with the barley and the vegetables, the squash, mustard, and cucumber——
> As squashes add them to the number.

Next they predict a man will die and one does in Transylvania, or the vineyards shall suffer drought, or people take to beer in far-off Germany; also cherries will freeze and impoverish the neighbors in Gascony, while there will be a plague of tigers in Hyrcania. So or not so, pray remember
> The year ends with December.

(LEONELO, *a student, enters with* BARRILDO)

LEONELO: I grant this town nothing, upon a re-view, but as the plain seat of stupidity.

BARRILDO: How did you fare in Salamanca?

LEONELO: That is no simple story.
BARRILDO: By this you must be a complete Bártulo.
LEONELO: Not even a barber by this. In our faculty few tri[m]
knowledge from the course.
BARRILDO: You return to us a scholar.
LEONELO: No, but I have learned what it is wise to know.
BARRILDO: With all the printing of books nowadays a ma[n]
might pick up a few and be wise.
LEONELO: We know less than we did when there was les[s]
knowledge, for the bulk of learning is so great no man ca[n]
compass it. Confusion results from excess, all the stir goe[s]
to froth, while those who read befuddle their heads wit[h]
endless pages and become literal slaves. The art of print[-]
ing has raised up a thousand geniuses over night. To b[e]
sure it spreads and conserves the Holy Scriptures, that the[y]
may be known of all and endure, but this invention o[f]
Guttenberg, that famous German of Mayence, has in fac[t]
devitalized glory. Many a man of repute has proved a ver[y]
fool when his books have been printed, or else suffere[d]
the mortification of having simpletons issue theirs in hi[s]
name. Others have set down arrant nonsense and credite[d]
it to their enemies out of spite, to whose undoing it circu[-]
lates and appals the world.
BARRILDO: I can find no words to argue with you.
LEONELO: The ignorant have the learned at their mercy.
BARRILDO: Leonelo, on every account printing is a might[y]
invention.
LEONELO: For centuries the world did very well without it[,]
and to this hour it has not produced one Jerome nor a sec[-]
ond Augustine. The men were saints.
BARRILDO: Sit down and rest, for my head is dizzy opposin[g]
you.

(JUAN ROJO *and a* FARMER *enter*)

JUAN ROJO: There is not a dower on four of these farms if th[e]
fields continue as they are, and this may be seen on all sides[,]
far and near, for all is one.
FARMER: What word of the Commander?
JUAN ROJO: Would Laurencia had never set foot by the river[.]

## The Sheep Well

FARMER: I could dangle him gladly from that olive-tree, savage, unbridled and lewd!

(*The* COMMANDER *enters with* ORTUÑO *and* FLORES)

COMMANDER: Heaven for the just!

REGIDOR: Commander!

COMMANDER: God's body, why do you stand?

ESTEBAN: Señor, where the custom is to sit, we stand.

COMMANDER: I tell you to sit down.

ESTEBAN: As honorable men we cannot do you honor, having none.

COMMANDER: Sit down while I talk with you!

ESTEBAN: Shall we discuss my hound, sir?

COMMANDER: Alcalde, these true men of mine praise the rare virtue of the animal.

ESTEBAN: The beast is swift. In God's name but he can overtake a thief or harry a coward right cruelly.

COMMANDER: I would set him on a graceful hare that these days lopes before me.

ESTEBAN: Done, if you will lead us to the hare.

COMMANDER: Oh, speaking of your daughter——

ESTEBAN: My daughter?

COMMANDER: Yes, why not? The hare.

ESTEBAN: My daughter is not your quarry.

COMMANDER: Alcalde, pray you prevail upon her.

ESTEBAN: How?

COMMANDER: She plumes herself before me. A wife, and a proud one, of a councillor who attends before me now, and listens, at my every look darts kindling glances.

ESTEBAN: She does ill. You, Señor, do ill also, speaking thus freely.

COMMANDER: Oh, what rustic virtue! Here, Flores, get him the book of *Politics*, and let him perfect himself in Aristotle.

ESTEBAN: Señor, the town would live in the reflection of your honor. There be men in Fuente Ovejuna.

LEONELO: I never read of such a tyrant.

COMMANDER: What have I said, in faith, to which you take exception, Regidor?

Juan Rojo: You have spoken ill. Speak well, for it is not meet you level at our honor.

Commander: Your honor? Good! Are we importing friars to Calatrava?

Regidor: There be those that be content to wear the cross, though the heart be not too pure.

Commander: I do not injure you, mingling my blood with yours.

Juan Rojo: A smirch is no hidden stain.

Commander: In doing my will I accord your wives honor.

Esteban: The very words spell dishonor, while your deeds pass all remedy.

Commander: Obstinate dolt! Ah, better the cities where men of parts and renown wreak their will and their pleasure! There husbands give thanks when their wives sacrifice upon the altar.

Esteban: They do no such service, if with this you would move us. God rules, too, in the cities, and justice is swift.

Commander: Get up and get out.

Esteban: We have said what you have heard.

Commander: Out of the square straight! Let not one remain behind!

Esteban: We firmly take our leave.

Commander: What? In company?

Flores: By the rood, hold your hand!

Commander: These hinds would slander me, defiling the square with lies, departing together.

Ortuño: Pray be patient.

Commander: I marvel that I am so calm! Walk each one by himself, apart. Let no man speak till his door has shut behind him!

Leonelo: Great God, can they stomach this?

Esteban: My path lies this way.

(Esteban, Juan Rojo, Regidor, Leonelo *and the* Peasants *go out, leaving the* Commander, Flores *and* Ortuño)

Commander: What shall we do with these knaves?

## The Sheep Well

ORTUÑO: Their speech offends you and you by no means hide your unwillingness to hear it.

COMMANDER: Do they compare themselves with me?

FLORES: Perversity of man.

COMMANDER: Shall that peasant retain my cross-bow and not be punished while I live?

FLORES: Last night we took him, as we thought, at Laurencia's door, and I gave an oaf who was his double a slash that married his two ears.

COMMANDER: Can you find no trace of that Frondoso?

FLORES: They say he remains in these parts still.

COMMANDER: And dares remain, who has attempted my life?

FLORES: Like a silly bird or a fish, a decoy will tempt him and he will fall into the lure.

COMMANDER: That a laborer, a stripling of the soil should aim a cross-bow at a captain before whose sword Córdoba and Granada tremble! Flores, the end of the world has come!

FLORES: Blame love, for it knows no monopoly of daring.

ORTUÑO: Seeing he lived, I took it as a token of your kindly disposition.

COMMANDER: Ortuño, the smile is false. Dirk in hand, within these two hours would I ransack the place, but vengeance yields the rein to reason until the hour shall come. Which of you had a smile of Pascuala?

FLORES: She says she intends to marry.

COMMANDER: How far is she prepared to go?

FLORES: She will advise you anon when she can accept a favor.

COMMANDER: How of Olalla?

ORTUÑO: Fair words.

COMMANDER: Buxom and spirited! How far?

ORTUÑO: She says her husband has been uneasy these past days, suspicious of my messages, and of your hovering about, attended. As soon as his fears are allayed, you shall have a sign.

COMMANDER: On the honor of a knight 'tis well! These rustics have sharp eyes and commonly are evil-minded.

ORTUÑO: Evil-minded, ill-spoken and ill-favored.

COMMANDER: Say not so of Inés.

FLORES: Which one?

COMMANDER: Antón's wife. Aha!

FLORES: Yes, she will oblige any day. I saw her in the corral, which you can enter secretly.

COMMANDER: These easy girls we requite but poorly. Flores, may women never learn the worth of the wares they sell!

FLORES: No pain wipes out the sweetness wholly. To prevail quickly, cheats the expectation, but, as philosophers agree, women desire the men as they are desired, nor can form be without substance, at which we should not complain, nor wonder.

COMMANDER: A man who is fiercely swept by love finds solace in a speedy yielding to desire, but afterward despises the object, for the road to forgetfulness, even under the star of honor, is to hold oneself cheap before love's importuning.

(CIMBRANOS, *a Soldier, enters, armed*)

CIMBRANOS: Where is the Commander?

ORTUÑO: Behold him, if you have the faculty of sight.

CIMBRANOS:
 Oh, gallant Fernán Gómez,
 Put off the rustic cap
 For the morion of steel
 And change the cloak
 For armor!
 The Master of Santiago
 And the Count of Cabra,
 By title of the Castilian Queen,
 Lay siege to Don Rodrigo Girón
 In Ciudad Real,
 And short his shrift unaided
 Before their approaching powers,
 Forfeiting the spoils so dearly won
 At cost of blood of Calatrava.
 Already from the battlements
 Our sentinels descry
 Pennons and banners,
 The castles and the lions,
 Quartered with the bars of Aragon.

## The Sheep Well

What though the King of Portugal
Heap on Girón vain honors?
Vanquished, the Master must creep home
To Almagro, wounded,
Abandoning the city.
To horse, to horse, Señor!
At sight of you
The enemy will fly
Headlong into Castile,
Nor pause this side surrender.

COMMANDER: Hold and speak no more!
Stay for me.
Ortuño, sound the trumpet
Here in the square.
What soldiers
Are billeted with me?

ORTUÑO: A troop of fifty men.

COMMANDER: To horse every one!

CIMBRANOS: Spur apace or Ciudad Real
Falls to the King

COMMANDER: That shall never be.

(*Exeunt*)

(*Open country, fields or meadow.*)

(MENGO *enters with* LAURENCIA *and* PASCUALA, *running*)

PASCUALA: Don't leave us.

MENGO: What's the matter?

LAURENCIA: Mengo, we seek the village in groups, when there's no man to go with us, for fear of the Commander.

MENGO: How can the ugly devil torment so many?

LAURENCIA: He is upon us night and day.

MENGO: Oh, would heaven send a bolt to strike him where he stands!

LAURENCIA: He's an unchained beast, poison, arsenic and pestilence throughout the land.

MENGO: Laurencia, they say Frondoso pointed an arrow at his breast for your sake, here in this very meadow.

LAURENCIA: Mengo, I hated all men till then, but since that day I relent. Frondoso had courage; it will cost him his life.

MENGO: He must fly these fields, that's sure.

LAURENCIA: I love him enough to advise it, but he'll have no counsel of me, storming and raging and turning away. The Commander swears he will hang him feet upward.

PASCUALA: I say hang the Commander.

MENGO: Stone him I say. God knows but I will up and at him with a rock I saved at the sheep-fold that will land him a crack that will crush his skull in! He's wickeder than Gabalus that old Roman.

LAURENCIA: The one that was so wicked was Heliogabalus. He was a man.

MENGO: Whoever he was, call him Gab or Gal, his scurvy memory yields to this. You know history. Was there ever a man like Fernán Gómez?

PASCUALA: No, he's no man. There must be tigers in him.

(JACINTA *enters*)

JACINTA: Help in God's name, if you are women!

LAURENCIA: Why, what's this, Jacinta?

PASCUALA: We are all your friends.

JACINTA: The Commander's men, on their way to Ciudad Real, armed with villainy when it should be steel, would seize me and take me to him.

LAURENCIA: God help you, Jacinta! With you, pray he be merciful, but I choose rather to die than be taken!
(*Exit*)

PASCUALA: Jacinta, being no man I cannot save you.
(*Exit*)

MENGO: I can because I am a man in strength and in name. Jacinta, stand beside me.

JACINTA: Are you armed?

MENGO: Twice. I have two arms.

JACINTA: You will need more.

MENGO: Jacinta, the ground bears stones.

(FLORES *and* ORTUÑO *enter*)

## The Sheep Well

FLORES: Did you think you could run away from us?

JACINTA: Mengo, I am dead with fear!

MENGO: Friends, these are poor peasant girls.

ORTUÑO: Do you assume to defend her?

MENGO: I do, so please you, since I am her relative and must protect her, if that may be.

FLORES: Kill him straightway!

MENGO: Strike me heaven, but I am in a rage! You can put a cord around my neck but, by God, I'll sell my life dear!

(*The* COMMANDER *and* CIMBRANOS *enter*)

COMMANDER: Who calls? What says this turd?

FLORES: The people of this town, which we should raze for there is no health in it, insult our arms.

MENGO: Señor, if pity can prevail in the face of injustice, reprove these soldiers who would force this peasant girl in your name, though spouse and parents be bred to honor, and grant me license straight to lead her home unharmed.

COMMANDER: I will grant them license straight to harm you for your impudence. Let go that sling.

MENGO: Señor——

COMMANDER: Flores, Ortuño and Cimbranos, it will serve to tie his hands.

MENGO: Is this the voice of honor?

COMMANDER: What do these sheep of Fuente Ovejuna think of me?

MENGO: Señor, have I offended you, or mayhap the village, in anything?

FLORES: Shall we kill him?

COMMANDER: It would soil your arms which we shall stain with redder blood.

ORTUÑO: We wait your orders, sir.

COMMANDER: Flog him without mercy. Tie him to that oak-tree, baring his back, and with the reins——

MENGO: No, no, for you are noble!

COMMANDER: Flog him till the rivets start from the straps!

MENGO: My God, can such things be?

(*They lead him off*)

COMMANDER: Pretty peasant, draw near daintily. Who would prefer a farmer to a valiant nobleman?

JACINTA: But will you heal my honor, taking me for yourself?

COMMANDER: Truly I do take you.

JACINTA: No, I have an honorable father, sir, who may not equal you in birth, but in virtue he is the first.

COMMANDER: These are troubled days nor will this rude peasantry salve my outraged spirit. Pass with me under the trees.

JACINTA: I?

COMMANDER: This way.

JACINTA: Look what you do!

COMMANDER: Refuse and I spurn you. You shall be the slut of the army.

JACINTA: No power of lust can overcome me.

COMMANDER: Silence and go before.

JACINTA: Pity, Señor!

COMMANDER: Pity have I none.

JACINTA: I appeal from your wickedness to God!

(*Exit the* COMMANDER, *hauling her out*)


(*Room in Juan Rojo's house.*)

(LAURENCIA *and* FRONDOSO *enter*)

LAURENCIA: Through fields of danger
　　　　　　My love comes to me.
FRONDOSO: The hazard bear witness
　　　　　　To the love that I bear.
　　　　　　The Commander has vanished
　　　　　　O'er the brow of the hill
　　　　　　And I, the slave of beauty,
　　　　　　Lose all sense of fear,
　　　　　　Seeing him disappear.
LAURENCIA: Speak ill of no man.
　　　　　　To pray for his end
　　　　　　Postpones it, my friend.

# The Sheep Well

FRONDOSO: Eternally.
And may he live a thousand years,
And every one bear joy!
I'll pray for his soul also
And may the pious litany
Bite, sear and destroy!
Laurencia, if my love
Live in your heart,
Let me enter there, love,
To dwell loyally.
The town counts us one,
Yet by the book we are twain.
Will you, I wonder,
Say yes,
Compulsion under?

LAURENCIA: Say for me to the town
Oh yes, yes and yes
Again and again!

FRONDOSO: I kiss your feet
For this new miracle of mercy.
Beauty grants me joy
In words grace conjures.

LAURENCIA: Flatter me no more,
But speak to my father
And win my uncle's praise.
Oh, speak,
Frondoso,
Oh may we marry, oh Frondoso,
It will be heaven
To be your wife!

FRONDOSO: In God we trust. (*Hides himself*)
(*Enter* ESTEBAN *and* JUAN ROJO, *Regidor*)

ESTEBAN: His departure outraged the square, and indeed it was most unseemly behavior. Such tyranny stuns as a blow; even poor Jacinta must pay the price of his madness.

JUAN ROJO: Spain turns already to the Catholic Kings, a name by which our rulers have come to be known, and the nation renders obedience to their laws. They have appointed the

Master of Santiago Captain General of Ciudad Real, despatching him forthwith against Girón's oppression of the town. But my heart aches for Jacinta, being as she is an honest girl.

ESTEBAN: They beat Mengo soundly.

JUAN ROJO: I never saw dye, black or red, to rival his flesh.

ESTEBAN: Peace and no more, for my blood boils, or else congeals at his name. Have I authority or a staff of office?

JUAN ROJO: The man cannot control his servants.

ESTEBAN: On top of all this they chanced on Pedro Redondo's wife one day in the very bottom of the valley, and after he insulted her she was turned over to the men.

JUAN ROJO: Who is listening concealed?

FRONDOSO: I, a petitioner.

JUAN ROJO: Granted, Frondoso. Your father brought you to be, but I have brought you to be what you are, a prop and support, who is my very son in the house.

FRONDOSO: Assured, Alcalde, of permission, I speak as one by birth honorable, and not obscure.

ESTEBAN: You have suffered wrong at the hand of Fernán Gómez?

FRONDOSO: More than a little.

ESTEBAN: My heart records it. The man is surely mad.

FRONDOSO: Señor, appealing to a father,
Serving a daughter,
I beg her hand
Not all a stranger.
Pardon presumption though it be extreme;
Boldly I speak for men shall count me bold.

ESTEBAN: By that word, Frondoso,
You renew my life,
Brushing aside
The apprehension of the years.
Now heaven be praised, my son,
For your proposal seals our honor,
Which may love guard jealously.
Apprise your father straight
Of this new promised joy,

## The Sheep Well

              For my consent stays
              But his approbation,
              In whose fair prospect
              Beams my happiness.

JUAN ROJO: The maid must consent also.

ESTEBAN:     Her consent should precede
              And has preceded indeed,
              Because a faithful lover
              Is prophet and recorder.

I have taken an oath to bestow some right good maravedis upon a good young man.

FRONDOSO: I seek no dower. Gold, they say, makes the day dull.

JUAN ROJO: So long as he does not court the wineskins, you may dower him without stint or mercy.

ESTEBAN: I will speak to my daughter that assurance may be doubly sure.

FRONDOSO: Do, pray, for violence has no part in love.

ESTEBAN: Dearest daughter Laurencia!

LAURENCIA: Oh, father?

ESTEBAN: She approves for she answers before I speak! Dearest daughter Laurencia, step apart a moment. Frondoso, who is an honest lad, if one there be in Fuente Ovejuna, inquires of me as to your friend Gila, whom he would honor as a wife.

LAURENCIA: Gila a wife?

ESTEBAN: Is she a fitting mate, a proper wife?

LAURENCIA: Yes, father, oh she is! Of course!

ESTEBAN: Of course she is ugly, as ugly as they come, which led me to suggest, Laurencia, that Frondoso look at you.

LAURENCIA: Father, be serious as becomes your office.

ESTEBAN: Do you love him?

LAURENCIA: I have favored him and am myself favored. But you knew!

ESTEBAN: Shall I say yes?

LAURENCIA: Yes, father, for me.

ESTEBAN: The yes will do for us both. Come, we will seek his father.

JUAN ROJO: Instantly.
ESTEBAN: My boy, to return to the dower. I can afford, ye
and I pledge, four thousand maravedis.
FRONDOSO: Señor, I am your son now and you offend me.
ESTEBAN: A day and pride abates, lad, but if you marry with
out a dower, by my faith, many a day will succeed and th
abatement not be mended.

(*Exeunt* ESTEBAN *and* JUAN ROJO)

LAURENCIA: Frondoso, bliss!
FRONDOSO:  Yes, triply.
    In a single moment
    I feel so happy
    I could die with pleasure!
    Bliss it must be
    Shared among three.
    I look at you and laugh,
    Laugh my heart out.
    Oh, what treasure
    I drink in at a glance
    Now love comes to me,
    Laurencia!

(*Exeunt*)


(*Ciudad Real. The walls.*)

(*The* MASTER, *the* COMMANDER,
FLORES *and* ORTUÑO *enter*)

COMMANDER: Fly, sir! There is no remedy.
MASTER: The wall giving way, the weight of the enemy un
does us.
COMMANDER: We have bled them and cost them many lives
MASTER: The banner of Calatrava shall not trail among thei
spoils, though it were recompense turning all to glory.
COMMANDER: Our league, Girón, crumbles and lies lifeless.
MASTER: Can we outstrip fortune, though she be blind, favor
ing us to-day, to-day to leave us?

## The Sheep Well

VOICES: (*Within*) Hail, Victory! Hail, the Crown of Castile!

MASTER: The pennons show upon the battlements while all the windows of the towers thrust banners forth, proclaiming the victory.

COMMANDER: Much joy may they have of the day! By my soul, a day of slaughter!

MASTER: Fernán Gómez, I'll to Calatrava.

COMMANDER: And I to Fuente Ovejuna. Stay upon your cousin of Portugal, or, weighing adversity, yield allegiance to the Catholic King.

MASTER: I shall apprise you with despatch.

COMMANDER: Time is a hard general.

MASTER: God grant me few years like this, fertile in undeception.

(*Exeunt*)

(*Esteban's house in Fuente Ovejuna.*)

(*Enter the wedding-train,* MUSICIANS, MENGO, FRONDOSO, LAURENCIA, PASCUALA, BARRILDO, ESTEBAN *and* JUAN ROJO)

MUSICIANS: *Joy to the bride*
*And long life beside!*
*Long life!*

MENGO: A clever boy thought that up! Oh, that boy is clever!

BARRILDO: He could troll it out at any wedding.

FRONDOSO: Mengo sings only to the lash because he says it has more tang to it.

MENGO: Yes, and I know a young chap in the valley, not meaning you of course, who would make a nice dish for the Commander.

BARRILDO: Enough of gloom and amen, seeing that a ferocious barbarian offers at our honor.

MENGO: I believe a hundred soldiers whipped me that day, and all I had was a sling that I gave up to protect me. How-

ever, I know a man, not mentioning names, who was full of
honor and pursued with a syringe loaded with dye and
some herbs that caused him great pain, and oh my, the pain
that they caused him! How that man did suffer!

BARRILDO: By way of jest. It was done as a laughing matter.

MENGO: As it came out afterwards. At the time he never
laughed nor even suspected, but felt much better without
the dye, though while it was in, death was preferable.

FRONDOSO: A song would be preferable, or anything. Come, let
it be a good one, Mengo.

MENGO: Good! Do you invite me?

MUSICIANS: *Bride and groom*
*Must dwell together.*
*Pray God neither one of them*
*Dare fight or row it.*
*Let both die*
*Just too tired out to live,*
*A long time after*
*They have forgotten all about it—*
*I mean the wedding.*

FRONDOSO: God help the poet who made that up!

BARRILDO: He needs more help.

MENGO: Oh, that reminds me! Did you ever see a baker bak-
ing buns? He dips the dough into the oil until the pot is
full, and then some swell up, some come out askew and
twisted, leaning to the right, tumbling to the left, some
scorched, some burned, some uneatable. Well, a poet's
subject is his dough, he plops a verse onto the paper hoping
it will turn out sweet, and his friends all tell him so, but
when he tries to sell it he has to eat it himself, for the world
is too wise to buy or else hasn't the money.

BARRILDO: You came to the wedding so as not to give the
bride and groom a chance to talk.

LAURENCIA: Uncle, you must be kissed. And you, too, Father—

# The Sheep Well

**Juan Rojo:** Not on the hand. May your father's hand be your protection, and Frondoso's also, in the hour of need.

**Esteban:** Rojo, heaven protect her and her husband on whom I invoke an everlasting benison.

**Frondoso:** Ever to share with you.

**Juan Rojo:** Come all now, play and sing, for they are as good as one.

**Musicians:**
*O maiden fair
With the flowing hair,
Shun Fuente Ovejuna!
A warrior knight
Awaits thee there,
Waits the maid with the flowing hair
With the Cross of Calatrava.
Oh, hide in the shade
By the branches made!
Why, lovely maiden,
Why afraid?
Against desire
No wall may aid
'Gainst the King of Calatrava.*

*Thou grim knight spare
Frail beauty there
By Fuente Ovejuna!
No screen can hide,
No mountain bare,
No ocean bar love anywhere
'Gainst the Knight of Calatrava.
Here in the shade,
Shall love's debt be paid.
O peerless maiden,
Why afraid?
Against desire
No wall may aid
'Gainst the Knight of Calatrava.*

(*The* COMMANDER, FLORES, ORTUÑO *and*
CIMBRANOS *enter*)

COMMANDER: Let all in the house stand still on pain of death

JUAN ROJO: Señor, though this be no play, your comman[d] shall be obeyed. Will you sit down? Why all these arm[s] and weapons? We question not, for you bring home victory

FRONDOSO: I am dead unless heaven helps me.

LAURENCIA: Stand behind me, Frondoso.

COMMANDER: No, seize and bind him.

JUAN ROJO: Surrender, boy, 'tis best.

FRONDOSO: Do you want them to kill me?

JUAN ROJO: Why, pray?

COMMANDER: I am no man to take life unjustly, for, if I were my soldiers would have run him through ere this, forward or rearwards. Throw him into prison where his own fathe[r] shall pronounce sentence upon him, chained in his dan[k] cell.

PASCUALA: This is a wedding, Señor.

COMMANDER: What care I for weddings? Is this your occupa[-] tion in the village?

PASCUALA: Pardon him, Señor, if he has done wrong, bein[g] who you are.

COMMANDER: Pascuala, he has done no wrong to me, bu[t] offense to the Master, Téllez Girón, whom God preserve[.] He has mocked his law, scoffed at his rule, and punishmen[t] must be imposed as a most dire example, or there will b[e] those to rise against the Master, seeing that one afternoon but shortly gone, flower of these loyal and faithful vassal[s,] he dared take aim, pointing the cross-bow at the bosom o[f] the High Commander.

ESTEBAN: If a father-in-law may offer a word of excuse, hi[s] dudgeon was not strange but manly, taking umbrage as lover. You would deprive him of his wife. Small wonder th[e] man should defend her!

COMMANDER: Alcalde, the truth is not in you.

ESTEBAN: Be just, Señor.

COMMANDER: I had no thought to deprive him of his wife, no[r] could so have done, he having none.

## The Sheep Well

ESTEBAN: But you had the thought, which shall suffice. Henceforth enough! A King and Queen rule now in Castile whose firm decrees shall bring this rioting to cease, nor will they stay their hands, these wars once ended, nor suffer arrogance to overpower their towns and villages, crucifying the people cruelly. Upon his breast the King will place a cross, and on that royal breast it shall be the symbol, too, of honor!

COMMANDER: Death to presumption! Wrest the staff from him.

ESTEBAN: Señor, I yield it up, commanded.

COMMANDER: Beat him with it while he capers about this stable. Have at him smartly!

ESTEBAN: Still we suffer your authority. I am ready. Begin!

PASCUALA: They beat an old man?

LAURENCIA: Yes, because he is my father. Beat him, avenging yourself on me!

COMMANDER: Arrest her, and let ten soldiers guard this sinful maid!

(*Exeunt* COMMANDER *and Train*)

ESTEBAN: Justice, descend this day from heaven!
(*Exit*)

PASCUALA: No wedding but a shambles.
(*Exit*)

BARRILDO: And not a man of us said a word!

MENGO: I have had my beating already and you can still see purple enough on me to outfit a Cardinal, without the trouble of sending to Rome. Try, if you don't believe it, what a thorough job they can do.

JUAN ROJO: We must all take counsel.

MENGO: My counsel, friends, is to take nothing but forget it. I know which side I am on, though I don't say, for it's scaled like a salmon. Never again will any man get me to take it! Nor woman either.

# ACT III

(*A room in the Town Hall at Fuente Ovejuna.*)

(ESTEBAN, ALONSO *and* BARRILDO *enter*)

ESTEBAN: Is the Town Board assembled?
BARRILDO: Not a person can be seen.
ESTEBAN: Bravely we face danger!
BARRILDO: All the farms had warning.
ESTEBAN: Frondoso is a prisoner in the tower and my daughter Laurencia in such plight that she is lost save for the direct interposition of heaven.

(JUAN ROJO *enters with the* SECOND REGIDOR)

JUAN ROJO: Who complains aloud when silence is salvation? Peace, in God's name, peace!
ESTEBAN: I will shout to the clouds till they re-echo my complaints while men marvel at my silence.

(*Enter* MENGO *and* PEASANTS)

MENGO: We came to attend the meeting.
ESTEBAN: Farmers of this village, an old man whose grey beard is bathed in tears, inquires what rites, what obsequies we poor peasants, assembled here, shall prepare for our ravished homes, bereft of honor? And if life be honor, how shall we fare since there breathes not one among us whom this savage has not offended? Speak! Who but has been wounded deeply, poisoned in respect? Lament now, yes, cry out! Well? If all be ill, how then say well? Well, there is work for men to do.
JUAN ROJO: The direst that can be. Since by report it is published that Castile is subject now to a King, who shall

presently make his entrance into Córdoba, let us despatch two Regidors to that city to cast themselves at his feet and demand remedy.

BARRILDO: King Ferdinand is occupied with the overthrow of his enemies, who are not few, so that his commitments are warlike entirely. It were best to seek other succor.

REGIDOR: If my voice have any weight, I declare the independence of the village.

JUAN ROJO: How can that be?

MENGO: On my soul, my back tells me the Town Board will be informed as to that directly.

REGIDOR: The tree of our patience has been cut down, the ship of our joy rides storm-tossed, emptied of its treasure. They have rept the daughter from one who is Alcalde of this town in which we dwell, breaking his staff over his aged head. Could a slave be scorned more basely?

JUAN ROJO: What would you have the people do?

REGIDOR: Die or rain death on tyrants! We are many while they are few.

BARRILDO: Lift our hands against our Lord and Master?

ESTEBAN: Only the King is our master, save for God, never these devouring beasts. If God be with us, what have we to fear?

MENGO: Gentlemen, I advise caution in the beginning and ever after. Although I represent only the very simplest laborers, who bear the most, believe me we find the bearing most unpleasant.

JUAN ROJO: If our wrongs are so great, we lose nothing with our lives. An end, then! Our homes and vineyards burn. Vengeance on the tyrants!

(*Enter* LAURENCIA, *her hair disheveled*)

LAURENCIA: Open, for I have need of the support of men! Deeds, or I cry out to heaven! Do you know me?

ESTEBAN: Martyr of God, my daughter?

JUAN ROJO: This is Laurencia.

LAURENCIA: Yes, and so changed that, gazing, you doubt still!

ESTEBAN: My daughter!

LAURENCIA: No, no more! Not yours.

ESTEBAN: Why, light of my eyes, why, pride of the valley?
LAURENCIA: Ask not, reckon not,
>Here be it known
>Tyrants reign o'er us,
>We are ruled by traitors,
>Justice is there none.
>I was not Frondoso's,
>Yours to avenge me,
>Father, till the night
>I was yours
>Though he was my husband,
>You the defender
>Guarding the bride.

As well might the noble pay for the jewel lost in the merchant's hand!

>I was lost to Fernán Gómez,
>Haled to his keep,
>Abandoned to wolves.
>A dagger at my breast
>Pointed his threats,
>His flatteries, insults, lies,
>To overcome my chastity
>Before his fierce desires.

My face is bruised and bloody in this court of honest men. Some of you are fathers, some have daughters. Do your hearts sink within you, supine and cowardly crew? You are sheep, sheep! Oh, well-named, Village of Fuente Ovejuna, the Sheep Well! Sheep, sheep, sheep! Give me iron, for senseless stones can wield none, nor images, nor pillars—jasper though they be—nor dumb living things that lack the tiger's heart that follows him who steals its young, rending the hunter limb from limb upon the very margin of the raging sea, seeking the pity of the angry waves.

>But you are rabbits, farmers,
>Infidels in Spain,
>Your wives strut before you
>With the cock upon their train!
>Tuck your knitting in your belts,

## The Sheep Well

        Strip off your manly swords,
        For, God living, I swear
        That your women dare
        Pluck these fearsome despots,
        Beard the traitors there!
        No spinning for our girls;
        Heave stones and do not blench.
        Can you smile, men?
        Will you fight?
        Caps we'll set upon you,
        The shelter of a skirt,
        Be heirs, boys, to our ribbons,
        The gift of the maidenry,

For now the Commander will hang Frondoso from a merlon of the tower, without let or trial, as presently he will string you all, you race of half-men, for the women will leave this village, nor one remain behind! To-day the age of amazons returns, we lift our arms and strike against this villainy, and the crash of our blows shall amaze the world!

ESTEBAN: Daughter, I am no man to bear names calmly, opprobrious and vile. I will go and beard this despot, though the united spheres revolve against me.

JUAN ROJO: So will I, for all his pride and knavery.

REGIDOR: Let him be surrounded and cut off.

BARRILDO: Hang a cloth from a pike as our banner and cry "Death to Monsters!"

JUAN ROJO: What course shall we choose?

MENGO: To be at them, of course. Raise an uproar and with it the village, for every man will take an oath and be with you that to the last traitor the oppressors shall die.

ESTEBAN: Seize swords and spears, cross-bows, pikes and clubs.

MENGO: Long live the King and Queen!

ALL: Live our lords and masters!

MENGO: Death to cruel tyrants!

ALL: To cruel tyrants, death!

    (*Exeunt all but* LAURENCIA)

LAURENCIA: March on, and heaven march before you!

*(At the door)*

Hello! Ho, women of this town! Draw near! Draw near for the salvation of your honor!

(PASCUALA, JACINTA *and various* WOMEN *enter*)

PASCUALA: Who calls us? Where are the men to-day?

LAURENCIA: Behold them down that street, marching to murder Fernán Gómez. Yes, old men, young men, and troops of eager boys, like furies run to meet him! Shall they share all the glory of this mighty day, when we women can boast wrongs that match and outstrip theirs?

JACINTA: What can we do?

LAURENCIA: Fall in behind me and we will do a deed that shall re-echo round the sphere! Jacinta, you have been most deeply wronged; lead forth a squadron of our girls.

JACINTA: You have borne no less.

LAURENCIA: Oh, Pascuala, for a flag!

PASCUALA: Tie a cloth upon this lance to flourish. We shall have our banner.

LAURENCIA: Stay not even for that, for now it comes to me:— Every woman her headdress! Wave, banners, wave!

PASCUALA: Name a captain and march!

LAURENCIA: We need no captain.

PASCUALA: No? Wave, banners!

LAURENCIA: When my courage is up I laugh at the Cid and pale Rodomonte!

*(Exeunt)*


*(Hall in the Castle of the Commander.)*

(FLORES, ORTUÑO, CIMBRANOS *and the*
COMMANDER *enter. Also* FRONDOSO, *his hands bound*)

COMMANDER: And by the cord that dangles from his hands Let him be hung until cut down by death.

FRONDOSO: My Lord, you shame your worth.

COMMANDER: String him up on the battlements without further word.

## The Sheep Well

FRONDOSO: I had no thought, my Lord, against your life.

FLORES: What is this noise outside?
   (*Noise and uproar*)

COMMANDER: I hear voices.

FLORES: Do they threaten your justice, sire?

ORTUÑO: They are breaking down the gates.
   (*Knocking and blows*)

COMMANDER: The gate of my castle, the seat of the Commandery?

FLORES: The people fill the court.

JUAN ROJO: (*Within*) Push, smash, pull down, burn, destroy!

ORTUÑO: I like not their numbers.

COMMANDER: Shall these hinds come against me?

FLORES: Such passing fury sweeps them that all the outer doors are already beaten in!

COMMANDER: Undo this bumpkin. Frondoso, speak to this Alcalde. Warn him of his peril.

FRONDOSO: Sire, what they do, remember is done in love.
   (*Exit*)

MENGO: (*Within*) Hail, Ferdinand and Isabella, and let the last traitor die!

FLORES: Señor, in God's name you had best conceal your person.

COMMANDER: If they persevere we can hold this room, for the doors are strong. They will turn back as quickly as they came.

FLORES: When the people rise and screw their courage to the point, they never stop short of rapine and blood.

COMMANDER: Behind this grating as a barricade we can defend ourselves right stoutly.

FRONDOSO: (*Within*) Free Fuente Ovejuna!

COMMANDER: What a leader for these swine! I will out and fall upon them.

FLORES: I marvel at your courage.

ESTEBAN: (*Entering*) Now we meet the tyrant and his minions face to face! Death to the traitor! All for Fuente Ovejuna!
   (*Enter the* PEASANTS)

COMMANDER: Hold, my people! Stay!

ALL: Wrongs hold not. Vengeance knows no stay!
COMMANDER: Tell your wrongs, and on the honor of a knight I'll requite them, every one.
ALL: Fuente Ovejuna! Long live Ferdinand, our King! Death to traitors and unbelievers!
COMMANDER: Will you not hear me? I lift my voice. I am your lord and master.
ALL: No, our lords and masters are the Catholic Kings!
COMMANDER: Stay a little.
ALL: All for Fuente Ovejuna! Die, Fernán Gómez!
  (*Exeunt after breaking through the bars. The* WOMEN *enter, armed*)
LAURENCIA: Stop here and challenge fortune, no women but an army.
PASCUALA: Any that shows herself a woman by mercy, shall swallow the enemy's blood!
JACINTA: We shall spit his body on our pikes.
PASCUALA: As one we stand behind you.
ESTEBAN: (*Within*) Die, traitor though Commander!
COMMANDER: I die! O God, have pity in Thy clemency!
BARRILDO: (*Within*) Flores next!
MENGO: Have at him, for he landed on me with a thousand whacks.
FRONDOSO: I'll draw his soul out like a tooth!
LAURENCIA: They need us there!
PASCUALA: Let them go on! We guard the door.
BARRILDO: (*Within*) No prayers, no mercy, vermin!
LAURENCIA: Pascuala, I go with my sword drawn, not sheathed!
  (*Exit*)
BARRILDO: (*Within*) Down with Ortuño!
FRONDOSO: Slash him across the cheek.
  (FLORES *enters, fleeing, pursued by* MENGO)
FLORES: Pity, Mengo! I was not to blame.
MENGO: To be a pimp was bad enough, but why the devil lay on me?
PASCUALA: Mengo, give this man to the women. Stay! Stay!

## The Sheep Well          57

MENGO: 'Fore God I will! And no punishment could be worse.
PASCUALA: Be well avenged!
MENGO: Believe me!
JACINTA: Run him through!
FLORES: What? Pity, women!
JACINTA: His courage well becomes him.
PASCUALA: So he has tears?
JACINTA: Kill him, viper of the vile!
PASCUALA: Down, wretch, and die!
FLORES: Pity, women, pity!

(ORTUÑO *enters, pursued by* LAURENCIA)

ORTUÑO: I am not the man, I was not guilty!
LAURENCIA: In, women, and dye your conquering swords in traitor's blood. Prove all your courage!
PASCUALA: Die dealing death!
ALL: All for Fuente Ovejuna! Hail, King Ferdinand!
(*Exeunt*)


(*Near Ciudad Real.*)


(*Enter the* KING DON FERDINAND OF ARAGON *and* QUEEN ISABELLA OF CASTILE, *accompanied by* DON MANRIQUE, *Master of Santiago*)

MANRIQUE: Convenient haste hard following on command,
   The victory was gained at little cost,
   With show of slight resistance. Eagerly
   We crave a fresh assault to try our prowess.
   The Count of Cabra consolidates the front
   And fends a counter-stroke, keeping the field.
KING: The troops are well disposed. By our decree
   He shall continue in his tents, the line
   Reforming, holding the pass. An evil wind
   Sweeps up from Portugal, where armed Alfonso
   Levies further powers. Cabra shall remain
   The head and forefront of our valor here,
   Watchful as diligent, that men may see

The danger fly before the sentinel
And peace return with plenty to the land.
   (*Enter* FLORES, *wounded*)
FLORES:  King Ferdinand the Catholic,
         By right acclaim in Castile crowned,
         In token of thy majesty
         Oh hear the foulest treachery
         Done yet by man from where the sun
         Springs in the wakening east
         To the lands of westering night!
KING:    If there be warrant, speak.
FLORES:  O thou great King, my wounds speak,
         Admitting no delay
         To close my story
         With my life.
         I come from Fuente Ovejuna,
         Where the wretched hinds of the village
         Have basely murdered their liege lord
         In one general mutiny.
         Perfidious folk,
         They slew Fernán Gómez
         As vassals moving upon slight cause,
         Fixing upon him
         The name of Tyrant,
         Thenceforward their excuse.
         They broke down his doors,
         Closing their ears
         To his free knightly pledge
         To do each and all
         Full justice,
         Steeling their hearts against him,
         And with unseemly rage
         Tearing the cross from his breast,
         Inflicting cruel wounds.
After which they cast him from a high window to the ground where he was caught on pikes and sword-points by the women. They bore him in dead and the most revengeful pulled at his beard and hair, defacing every feature, for

their fury waxed to such extremity that they sliced off his ears neatly. They beat down his scutcheon with staves and boast outright that they will set the royal arms above the portal where their lord's should be, full in the square of the village. They sacked the keep as a fallen foe's, and, exulting, raped his goods and properties. These things I saw, hidden —unhappy was my lot!—and so remained till nightfall, escaping to lay my prayer before you. Justice, Sire, that swift penalty may fall upon these offending churls! Bloodshed this day cries out to God and challenges your rigor!

KING: No violence, no cruelty so dire
Escapes the inquest of our royal eye.
I marvel greatly at this villainy,
Wherefore to-day a judge shall be despatched
To verify the tale, and punishment
Mete out unto the guilty as example.
A captain, too, shall march in his escort
Securing the sentence, for mutiny
The bolder grown, bolder the chastisement.
Look to his wounds.

(*Exeunt*)


(*The Square in Fuente Ovejuna.*)

(*The* PEASANTS *enter, men and women, bearing the head of* FERNAN GÓMEZ *on a pike*)

MUSICIANS:     *Hail, Ferdinand!*
               *Isabella, hail!*
               *Death, tyrant band!*

BARRILDO: Let's hear from Frondoso.
FRONDOSO: I've made a song and, if it's wrong,
  You correct it as it goes along.

               *Hail, Isabella!*
               *'Tis plain to be seen*

> *Two can make one,*
> *A King and a Queen.*
> *When they die—*
> *This to you, Saint Michael—*
> *Just lift them both up to the sky.*
> *Sweep the land clean,*
> *O King and Queen!*

LAURENCIA: See what you can do, Barrildo.
BARRILDO: Silence, then, while I get a rhyme in my head.
PASCUALA: If you keep your head it will be twice as good.
BARRILDO: *Hail to the King and Queen,*
*For they are very famous!*
*They have won*
*And so they will not blame us.*
*May they always win,*
*Conquer giants*
*And a dwarf or two.*
*Down with tyrants!*
*And now I'm through.*

MUSICIANS: *Hail, Ferdinand!*
*Isabella, hail!*
*Death, tyrant band!*

LAURENCIA: Mengo next!
FRONDOSO: Now Mengo!
MENGO: I'm a poet that is one.
PASCUALA: You're the back of the belly.

MENGO: *Oh, one Sunday morning*
*The rascal beat me*
*From behind!*
*'Twas no way to treat me,*
*Most unkind.*
*How it hurt to seat me!*
*Glory to the Christian Kings!—*
*The wife must mind.*

## The Sheep Well

MUSICIANS:
        *Hail, Ferdinand!*
        *Isabella, hail!*
        *Death, tyrant band!*

ESTEBAN: You can take the head off the spear now.

MENGO: He might have been hung for his looks. Phew!

    (JUAN ROJO *enters with a shield bearing the royal arms*)

REGIDOR: Here come the arms!

ESTEBAN: Let all the people see.

JUAN ROJO: Where shall the arms be set?

REGIDOR: Before the town-hall, here, above the door.

ESTEBAN: Noble escutcheon, hail!

BARRILDO: That is a coat of arms!

FRONDOSO: I see the light to-day, for the sun begins to shine.

ESTEBAN:    Hail Castile and hail León!
        Hail the bars of Aragon!
            May tyrants die!
        Hear, Fuente Ovejuna,
        Follow counsel of the wise,
            Nor hurt shall lie;
        King and Queen must needs inquire
        Right and wrong as they transpire,
            Passing near-by
        Loyalty our hearts inspire.

FRONDOSO: That's a problem too What shall our story be?

ESTEBAN: Let us all agree to die, if it must be, crying *Fuente Ovejuna*, and may no word of this affair pass beyond that ever.

FRONDOSO: Besides it is the truth, for what was done, Fuente Ovejuna did it, every man and woman.

ESTEBAN: Then that shall be our answer?

ALL: Yes!

ESTEBAN: Now I shall be the Judge and rehearse us all in what we best had do. Mengo, put you to the torture first.

MENGO: Am I the only candidate?

ESTEBAN: This is but talk, lad.

MENGO: All the same let's get through with it, and quickly.

ESTEBAN: Who killed the Commander?
MENGO: Fuente Ovejuna killed him.
ESTEBAN: I'll put you to the torture.
MENGO: You will on your life, sir.
ESTEBAN: Confess, conscienceless hind!
MENGO: I do. What of it?
ESTEBAN: Who killed the Commander?
MENGO: Fuente Ovejuna.
ESTEBAN: Rack him again! Turn the wheel once more.
MENGO: You oblige me.
ESTEBAN: Reduce him to carrion and let him go.

(*Enter* CUADRADO, *Regidor*)

CUADRADO: What is this meeting?
FRONDOSO: Why so grave, Cuadrado?
CUADRADO: The King's Judge is here.
ESTEBAN: All to your homes, and quickly!
CUADRADO: A Captain comes with him also.
ESTEBAN: Let the devil appear! You know what you are to say.
CUADRADO: They are going through the village prepared to take a deposition of every soul.
ESTEBAN: Have no fear.—Mengo, who killed the Commander?
MENGO: Fuente Ovejuna. Ask me who!

(*Exeunt*)


(*Almagro. A room in the Castle.*)

(*The* MASTER *enters with a* SOLDIER)

MASTER: Such news cannot be! To end like this? I have a mind to run you through for your insolence.
SOLDIER: I was sent, Master, without malice.
MASTER: Can a mad handful of louts be moved to such fury? I will take five hundred men forthwith and burn the village, leaving no memory of those paths that were so basely trod.
SOLDIER: Master, be not so moved, for they have committed themselves to the King, whose power is not to be gainsaid lightly.

# The Sheep Well

MASTER: How can they commit themselves to the King when they are vassals of Calatrava?

SOLDIER: That, Master, you will discuss with the King.

MASTER: No, for the land is his and all that it contains. I do obeisance to the Crown, and if they have submitted to the King I will subdue my rage and betake me to his presence as to a father's. My fault is grievous, in whose palliation I plead my untried years. I hang my head at this mischance of honor, but again to stumble were clear dishonor, yes, and certain death.

(*Exeunt*)


(*The Square of Fuente Ovejuna.
Before the Town Hall.*)

(*Enter* LAURENCIA)

LAURENCIA: Loving, that the beloved should suffer pain
  A grinding sorrow fastens on the heart,
Fearing the loved must bear alone the smart
  Care weighs the spirit down and hope lies slain.
  The firm assurance, watchful to attain,
Doubting falters, and hastens to depart,
Nor is it folly in the brave to start
  And tremble, promised boon transformed to bane.
I love my husband dearly. Now I see
Harpies of Vengeance rise before my sight
  Unshapely, and my hope breathes a faint breath.
Only his good I seek. Oh, set him free
  Ever with me to tremble in the night,
  Or take him from me, so you take me, death!

(*Enter* FRONDOSO)

FRONDOSO: Linger not, Laurencia.

LAURENCIA: My dear husband, fly danger, for I am its very heart.

FRONDOSO: Are you one to reject the homage of a lover?

LAURENCIA: My love, I fear for you, and you are my constant care.

FRONDOSO: Laurencia, I am so happy that surely this moment heaven smiles upon us both.

LAURENCIA: You see what has happened to the others, and how this judge proceeds firmly, with all severity? Save yourself before it is too late. Fly and avoid the danger!

FRONDOSO: What do you expect in such an hour? Shall I disappear and leave the peril to others, besides absenting myself from your sight? No, counsel me courage, for in danger a man betrays his blood, which is as it should be, come what may.

(*Cries within*)

I hear cries. They have put a man to the torture unless my ears deceive me. Listen and be still!

(*The* JUDGE *speaks within and Voices are heard in response*)

JUDGE: Old man, I seek only the truth. Speak!

FRONDOSO: An old man tortured?

LAURENCIA: What barbarity!

ESTEBAN: Ease me a little.

JUDGE: Ease him. Who killed Fernando?

ESTEBAN: Fuente Ovejuna.

LAURENCIA: Good, father! Glory and praise!

FRONDOSO: Praise God he had the strength!

JUDGE: Take that boy there. Speak, you pup, for you know! Who was it? He says nothing. Put on the pressure there.

BOY: Judge, Fuente Ovejuna.

JUDGE: Now by the King, carls, I'll hang you to the last man! Who killed the Commander?

FRONDOSO: They torture the child and he replies like this?

LAURENCIA: There is courage in the village.

FRONDOSO: Courage and heart.

JUDGE: Put that woman in the chair. Give her a turn for her good.

LAURENCIA: I can't endure it.

JUDGE: Peasants, be obstinate and this instrument brings death. So prepare! Who killed the Commander?

# The Sheep Well

PASCUALA: Judge, Fuente Ovejuna.
JUDGE: Have no mercy.
FRONDOSO: I cannot think, my mind is blank!
LAURENCIA: Frondoso, Pascuala will not tell them.
FRONDOSO: The very children hold their peace!
JUDGE: They thrive upon it.—More! More!
PASCUALA: Oh, God in heaven!
JUDGE: Again, and answer me! Is she deaf?
PASCUALA: I say Fuente Ovejuna.
JUDGE: Seize that plump lad, half undressed already.
LAURENCIA: It must be Mengo! Poor Mengo!
FRONDOSO: He can never hold out.
MENGO: Oh, oh, oh!
JUDGE: Let him have it.
MENGO: Oh!
JUDGE: Prod his memory.
MENGO: Oh, oh!
JUDGE: Who slew the Commander, slave?
MENGO: Oh, oh! I can't get it out! I'll tell you——
JUDGE: Loosen that hand.
FRONDOSO: We are lost!
JUDGE: Let him have it on the back!
MENGO: No, for I'll give up everything!
JUDGE: Who killed him?
MENGO: Judge, Fuente Ovejuna.
JUDGE: Have these rogues no nerves that they can laugh at pain? The most likely, too, lie by instinct. I will no more to-day. To the street!
FRONDOSO: Now God bless Mengo! I was afraid, transfixed, but that lad is a cure for fear.

(BARRILDO *and the* REGIDOR *enter with* MENGO)

BARRILDO: Good, Mengo, good!
REGIDOR: You have delivered us.
BARRILDO: Mengo, bravo!
FRONDOSO: We cheer you.
MENGO: Oh, oh! Not much.
BARRILDO: Drink, my friend, and eat. Come, come!

MENGO: Oh, oh! What have you got?
BARRILDO: Sweet lemon peel.
MENGO: Oh, oh!
FRONDOSO: Drink, drink. Take this.
BARRILDO: He does, too.
FRONDOSO: He takes it well. Down it goes.
LAURENCIA: Give him another bite.
MENGO: Oh, oh!
BARRILDO: Drink this for me.
LAURENCIA: Swallowed without a smile.
FRONDOSO: A sound answer deserves a round drink.
REGIDOR: Another, son?
MENGO: Oh, oh! Yes, yes!
FRONDOSO: Drink, for you deserve it.
LAURENCIA: He collects for every pang.
FRONDOSO: Throw a coat around him or he will freeze.
BARRILDO: Have you had enough?
MENGO: No, three more. Oh, oh!
FRONDOSO: He is asking for the wine.
BARRILDO: Yes, let him drink as much as he likes for one good turn begets another. What's the matter now?
MENGO: It leaves a taste in my mouth. Oh, I'm catching cold!
FRONDOSO: Another drink will help. Who killed the Commander?
MENGO: Fuente Ovejuna.
   (*Exeunt the* REGIDOR, MENGO *and* BARRILDO)
FRONDOSO: He has earned more than they give him. Ah, love, as you are mine confess to me. Who killed the Commander?
LAURENCIA: Love, Fuente Ovejuna.
FRONDOSO: Who?
LAURENCIA: Don't you think you can torture me. Fuente Ovejuna.
FRONDOSO: It did? How did I get you, then?
LAURENCIA: Love, I got you.
   (*Exeunt*)

## The Sheep Well

(*The open country.*)

(*Enter the* KING *and* QUEEN, *meeting*)

ISABELLA: Meeting, Sire, we crown our fortunes gladly.
KING: In union lies a more enduring glory.
 Passing to Portugal the direct path
 Leads me to you.
ISABELLA: To my heart, Majesty,
 Turning away from conquest gratefully.
KING: What news of the war in Castile?
ISABELLA: Peace succeeds and the land lies ready, expecting the plough.
KING: Now my eyes light upon a living miracle, the consummation of a queenly peace.
 (*Enter* DON MANRIQUE)
MANRIQUE: The Master of Calatrava begs audience, having journeyed to your presence from his seat.
ISABELLA: I have a mind to greet this gentleman.
MANRIQUE: Majesty, his years are few, yet they have proved his valor great.
 (*Exit*)
 (*Enter* THE MASTER)
MASTER: Rodrigo Téllez Girón,
 Master of Calatrava,
 Humbly kneels repentant
 And pardon begs, foredone.
 False counsels proffered one
 By one seduced my heart
 To deeds disloyal and rash;
 Now end all as begun
 When a too ready ear
 In Fernando placed its trust,
 That false and unjust knight.
 Pardon, Sire, past fear!
 In mercy hold me dear,
 Oh grant me royal favor,
 To pay in loyalty

>   Forever rendered here!
>   Upon Granada's plain
>   When sounds the wild alarm
>   My valor shall wreak harm,
>   My sword-strokes fall amain
>   And through that fell champaign
>   Dart wounds to the enemy
>   Till the cross of victory
>   Red o'er the merlons reign.
>   Five hundred men in steel
>   I shall lead to smite your foes
>   Upon my life and oath, or close
>   My eyes in death! Here I kneel,
>   Never to displease you more.

KING: Rise, Master. Having tendered your allegiance you shall be received royally.

MASTER: Every word is balm.

ISABELLA: Few speak as bravely as they fight.

MASTER: Esther has returned to earth to wed a Christian Xerxes.

(DON MANRIQUE *enters*)

MANRIQUE: Sire, the Judge that was despatched to Fuente Ovejuna has arrived with the process to report to Your Majesty.

KING: (*To the* MASTER) These aggressors, being of the Commandery, fall within your province.

MASTER: Sire, I yield to you, else were bloody vengeance taken for the death of the Commander.

KING: (*To the* QUEEN) Then the decision rests with me?

ISABELLA: I grant it willingly though the right were mine of God.

(*Enter* JUDGE)

JUDGE: I journeyed to Fuente Ovejuna in prosecution of your command probing all with due diligence and care. Having verified the crime, no writ or indictment has issued, inasmuch as with one accord and most singular fortitude, to all my questions as to the murderer the answer was always Fuente Ovejuna. Three hundred were put to torture, to the degree that forced them each to speak, without profit, Sire, of one word other than I have told you. Boys of ten were delivered to the rack, without yielding so much as a whisper, nor could they be moved by flattery or gold. Wherefore, this is my report, the evidence having failed: either you must pardon the village or wipe it out to the last man. They have followed me to your feet that in your own person you may pronounce judgment.

KING: If they seek our presence, let them appear before us, every one.

(*Enter* ESTEBAN *and* ALONSO, *Alcaldes,* JUAN ROJO *and* CUADRADO, *Regidors,* LAURENCIA, FRONDOSA, MENGO *and* PEASANTS, *both men and women*)

LAURENCIA: Are those the King and Queen?

FRONDOSO: The power and majesty of Castile!

LAURENCIA: How beautiful, how wonderful! Saint Antonio, bless them both!

ISABELLA: Are these the people of the village?

ESTEBAN: Majesty, Fuente Ovejuna humbly kneels at your feet in allegiance. The mad tyranny and fierce cruelty of the dead Commander, raining insults through the farms, themselves provoked his death. He ravished our homes, forced our daughters, and knew no heart nor mercy.

FRONDOSO: This simple girl, O Queen, who is mine by rite of heaven, and has brought me all happiness, which surely must be matchless, on my wedding-night, as if it had been his very own, he bore off to his keep, and but that she is secure in honor, basely that night he had deflowered her.

MENGO: I know something as to that, with your permission, Queen, because you must be anxious to hear from me, seeing the bloody tanning that I got. I stood up for a girl in the village when the Commander went along the way to her undoing, the scurvy Nero, and then he took it out on me, and there never was a more thorough job at bottom. Three men paid it their attention, good pay all three, since when, if you ask the explanation, I paid more for balm and ointment, with the powder and the myrtle I applied, than I could sell my sheep-cot for.

ESTEBAN: Sire, we yield ourselves to you. You are our King and in witness of submission we have placed your arms above our doors. Have mercy, Sire, for our excuse is our extremity, which deserves your clemency.

KING: As no indictment is set down, although the fault be grave, it shall be pardoned. Since you yield yourselves to me, I further take the town under my protection, for in the Crown henceforth its charter shall abide, until such time as God in His mercy shall vouchsafe you a new Commander.

FRONDOSO: When His Majesty speaks
    His voice we obey.
  "Fuente Ovejuna" ends.
    Friends, approve the play.

# LIFE IS A DREAM

# Calderon de la Barca

Pedro Calderón de la Barca (1600–1681) has been variously extolled by his admirers as "superior to Shakespeare" (the Frenchman, Paul Verlaine); "a dramatist who is at the head of the greatest in any language" (the American, James Russell Lowell); "the greatest Romantic dramatist of the past; a semi-God of the European drama; equaled perhaps only by Shakespeare" (the German, Friedrich Schlegel); "excelled in Spanish dramatic literature only by Lope" (various English critics); "ranks third after Sophocles and Shakespeare" (the Spaniard, Menéndez y Pelayo). Spanish literary critics maintain that if Lope was the founder of the national Spanish drama, Calderón consolidated it; that Lope excelled Calderón in creative power, naturalness and vivacity of dialogue, delicacy and charm of his heroines, and greater freshness of his theatre; but that Calderón excelled Lope in the vastness of his conceptions, profundity, sublimity, lyrism, polish and stagecraft. Nearly all literary historians agree that Lope was superior in comedy, Calderón in tragedy; and that Lope was more original, but Calderón was more artistic. Calderón was an intensely Spanish and profoundly religious writer, dominating his own age no less than Lope did the preceding one.

Calderón was born in Madrid and spent his early years in the study of law and philosophy at Salamanca. Later, in 1625, he entered the army. In the meantime, he had composed a number of dramas which were produced with considerable success, winning for him the praise of Lope de Vega. At the death of the latter, Calderón was summoned to Madrid by Philip IV, to whose Court he became attached as a master of revels. Ten years afterward he entered the priesthood, becoming a chaplain of honor to Philip. The "cloth" did not chill his ardor; and Calderón, like his predecessor, became entangled in the golden webs of Venus and Eros, and died, his friend, De Solís so charmingly put it—"as they say, t[he] swan dies, singing"—of love.

Calderón was a prodigious worker, his collected pla[ys] amounting to one hundred and twenty-two dramas, and abo[ut] twenty more theatrical pieces, chiefly religious in nature. [It] should be pointed out, however, that Lope wrote a doze[n] plays for every one of Calderón's. Of all his writings, the mo[st] famous is *La Vida Es Sueño* (*Life Is a Dream*), although *[La] Dama Duende* (*The Fair Lady*) was the playwright's favorit[e,] *El Alcalde de Zalamea* (*The Mayor of Zalamea*), his most i[m]portant play, and *La Devoción de la Cruz* (*Devotion to t[he] Cross*) his best religious play. His main themes are philosoph[y,] religion, intrigue and history. His supreme field was traged[y.] Much of his writing revolves around the trilogy of "Por [mi] Dios" (Religion), "por mi Rey" (Monarchy) and "por [mi] Dama" (Honor). His three chief concerns therefore were t[he] glorification of the Catholic church, the deification of t[he] Spanish sovereign as deriving his authority from divine orig[in] and guidance and the exaltation of womanhood as a vindic[a]tion of the *pundonor*, the highly developed and grossly a[nd] abhorrently exaggerated feeling for the point of honor. Mu[ch] of his work suffers from the stylistic plague of "*culteranism[o]*" or "*gongorismo*," a bombastic style replete with obscure hype[r]boles, far-fetched metaphors and strained phrases—an e[pi]demic which affected literatures of other countries as well [at] that time, e.g. "Marinism" in Italy, "Euphuism" in Englan[d,] "Schwulst" in Germany.

Without appraising the position of Calderón among gre[at] men of letters in and out of Spain, it can be conceded that [he] was a dramatic and lyric artist of very high rank—and tho[r]oughly Spanish. Evidences of both his shortcomings and vi[r]tues may be found in abundance in *Life Is a Dream*.

For further reading the following books are recommende[d:]

Fitzgerald, Edward, *Eight Dramas of Calderón*, New Yor[k,] 1921

Matthews, Brander, *The Chief European Dramatists*, Bo[s]ton, 1916

# Life Is a Dream
(*La Vida Es Sueño*)

*Life Is a Dream*, considered by many critics to be Calderón's most perfect work, is perhaps the best known Spanish play in this country. Its popularity is due to the fact that it is a beautifully poetic drama of ideas which embodies a lofty theme together with the typical elements of a well-constructed Spanish *comedia*.

The main plot, based on the tale of the awakened sleeper, deals with the philosophic struggle between free will and fate and the ultimate control of natural man through appeal to his obligations to his fellow-men. Calderón believes that our will is free. He compares life to a dream and concludes that even dreams are dreams. The sub-plots revolve around interesting and exciting palace-play intrigues, jealousy, love and honor—situations which are interwoven with skill and spirit. It might be added that one of the play's special appeals to English readers is the resemblance, in some respects, between the hero Sigismund and Shakespeare's Hamlet.

The play tells the story of the unfortunate Sigismund, prince of Poland, who was believed to have been born under an evil influence of the stars and was predestined to be a "most cruel" prince. We find him secluded in solitary confinement in a lonely forest cave with no contact with human beings other than Clotaldo, his old guardian. The prince was forced into this situation from earliest childhood by his father, King Basilius, in order to prevent the fulfillment of star-gazing soothsayers that the father would be disgraced and humiliated by the son. The king, in an effort to test Sigismund, has him narcotized and then brought to Court while in a trance. Awaking from his enforced sleep, Sigismund, who was brought up to live as a savage, finds himself in a sumptuous castle surrounded by luxuries and courtiers. As expected, he gives ve[nt] to his ferocious instincts and brutish traits, exploding wi[th] violence at the slightest irritation, hurling out of the windo[w] a courtier who dares to contradict him, and trying to assault [a] gentle maiden named Rosaura, the first female he has ev[er] seen. Basilius is thus convinced that it would be too dangero[us] for such an irresponsibly despotic and cruel son to succee[d] him to the throne. Drugging him again with a sleeping p[o]tion, he returns him to prison, leading him to believe when [he] awakens that the erstwhile experiences were only a dream.

The people rise up in defense of Sigismund whom the[y] consider to be the legitimate and rightful heir to the thron[e.] They vanquish his father, who forthwith sees himself hu[m]bled at his son's feet, in confirmation of the predicted fat[e.] However, thanks to his recent experiences, the prince displa[ys] a complete change in his character and behavior. He treats h[is] father with forgiveness and generosity, returning evil wi[th] good. Purged of animal passion, he marries off Rosaura to t[he] man of her choice. Thus, his free will overcomes all evil i[n]fluences, and he becomes in the end a mild and virtuo[us] sovereign, a model of self-restraint.

Even though the motif or thesis is not startlingly new, th[e] play is impressive not only because of the profound, symbol[ic] thought of the dénouement but also because of the grandio[se] majesty of the treatment and the poetic richness of th[e] language.

# LIFE IS A DREAM

# Characters

BASILIUS, *King of Poland*
SIGISMUND, *his son*
ASTOLFO, *Duke of Muscovy*
CLOTALDO, *a nobleman*
ESTRELLA, *a princess*
ROSAURA, *a lady*
CLARIN, *her servant*
Soldiers, Guards, Musicians, Attendants, Ladies, Servants

*The Scene is in the Court of Poland, in a fortress at some distance, and in the open field.*

# ACT I

(SCENE I. *At one side a craggy mountain, at the other a tower, the lower part of which serves as the prison of Sigismund. The door facing the spectators is half open. The action commences at nightfall*)

(ROSAURA *in man's attire appears on the rock heights and descends to the plain. She is followed by* CLARIN)

ROSAURA: Wild hippogriff swift speeding,
Thou that dost run, the wingéd winds exceeding,
Bolt which no flash illumes,
Fish without scales, bird without shifting plumes,
And brute awhile bereft
Of natural instinct, why to this wild cleft,
This labyrinth of naked rocks, dost sweep
Unreined, uncurbed, to plunge thee down the steep?
Stay in this mountain wold,
And let the beasts their Phaëton behold.
For I, without a guide,
Save what the laws of destiny decide,
Benighted, desperate, blind,
Take any path whatever that doth wind
Down this rough mountain to its base,
Whose wrinkled brow in heaven frowns in the sun's bright face.
Ah, Poland! in ill mood
Hast thou received a stranger, since in blood
The name thou writest on thy sands

    Of her who hardly here fares hardly at thy hands
    My fate may well say so:—
    But where shall one poor wretch find pity in her woe?
CLARIN: Say two, if you please;
    Don't leave me out when making plaints like these.
    For if we are the two
    Who left our native country with the view
    Of seeking strange adventures, if we be
    The two who, madly and in misery,
    Have got so far as this, and if we still
    Are the same two who tumbled down this hill,
    Does it not plainly to a wrong amount,
    To put me in the pain and not in the account?
ROSAURA: I do not wish to impart,
    Clarin, to thee, the sorrows of my heart;
    Mourning for thee would spoil the consolation
    Of making for thyself thy lamentation;
    For there is such a pleasure in complaining,
    That a philosopher I've heard maintaining
    One ought to seek a sorrow and be vain of it,
    In order to be privileged to complain of it.
CLARIN: That same philosopher
    Was an old drunken fool, unless I err:
    Oh, that I could a thousand thumps present him,
    In order for complaining to content him!
    But what, my lady, say,
    Are we to do, on foot, alone, our way
    Lost in the shades of night?
    For see, the sun descends another sphere to light.
ROSAURA: So strange a misadventure who has seen?
    But if my sight deceives me not, between
    These rugged rocks, half-lit by the moon's ray
    And the declining day,
    It seems, or is it fancy? that I see
    A human dwelling?
CLARIN: So it seems to me,
    Unless my wish the longed-for lodging mocks.
ROSAURA: A rustic little palace 'mid the rocks

## Life Is a Dream

Uplifts its lowly roof,
Scarce seen by the far sun that shines aloof.
Of such a rude device
Is the whole structure of this edifice,
That lying at the feet
Of these gigantic crags that rise to greet
The sun's first beams of gold,
It seems a rock that down the mountain rolled.

CLARIN: Let us approach more near,
For long enough we've looked at it from here;
Then better we shall see
If those who dwell therein will generously
A welcome give us.

ROSAURA: See an open door
(Funereal mouth 'twere best the name it bore),
From which as from a womb
The night is born, engendered in its gloom.
  (*The sound of chains is heard within*)

CLARIN: Heavens! what is this I hear?

ROSAURA: Half ice, half fire, I stand transfixed with fear.

CLARIN: A sound of chains, is it not?
Some galley-slave his sentence here hath got;
My fear may well suggest it so may be.

SIGISMUND (*in the tower*): Alas! Ah, wretched me!
Ah, wretched me!

ROSAURA: Oh what a mournful wail!
Again my pains, again my fears prevail.

CLARIN: Again with fear I die.

ROSAURA: Clarin!

CLARIN: My lady!

ROSAURA: Let us turn and fly
The risks of this enchanted tower.

CLARIN: For one,
I scarce have strength to stand, much less to run.

ROSAURA: Is not that glimmer there afar—
That dying exhalation—that pale star—
A tiny taper, which, with trembling blaze
Flickering 'twixt struggling flames and dying rays,

With ineffectual spark
Makes the dark dwelling place appear more dark?
Yes, for its distant light,
Reflected dimly, brings before my sight
A dungeon's awful gloom,
Say rather of a living corse, a living tomb;
And to increase my terror and surprise,
Dressed in the skins of beasts a man there lies:
A piteous sight,
Chained, and his sole companion this poor light.
Since then we cannot fly,
Let us attentive to his words draw nigh,
Whatever they may be.
  (*The doors of the tower open wide, and* SIGISMUND *is discovered in chains and clad in the skins of beasts. The light in the tower increases*)
SIGISMUND: Alas! Ah, wretched me! Ah, wretched me!
Heaven, here lying all forlorn,
I desire from thee to know,
Since thou thus dost treat me so,
Why have I provoked thy scorn
By the crime of being born?—
Though for being born I feel
Heaven with me must harshly deal,
Since man's greatest crime on earth
Is the fatal fact of birth—
Sin supreme without appeal.
This alone I ponder o'er,
My strange mystery to pierce through;
Leaving wholly out of view
Germs my hapless birthday bore,
How have I offended more,
That the more you punish me?
Must not other creatures be
Born? If born, what privilege
Can they over me allege
Of which I should not be free?
Birds are born, the bird that sings,

## Life Is a Dream

Richly robed by Nature's dower,
Scarcely floats—a feathered flower,
Or a bunch of blooms with wings—
When to heaven's high halls it springs,
Cuts the blue air fast and free,
And no longer bound will be
By the nest's secure control:—
And with so much more of soul,
Must I have less liberty?
Beasts are born, the beast whose skin
Dappled o'er with beauteous spots,
As when the great pencil dots
Heaven with stars, doth scarce begin
From its impulses within—
Nature's stern necessity,
To be schooled in cruelty,—
Monster, waging ruthless war:—
And with instincts better far
Must I have less liberty?
Fish are born, the spawn that breeds
Where the oozy seaweeds float,
Scarce perceives itself a boat,
Scaled and plated for its needs,
When from wave to wave it speeds,
Measuring all the mighty sea,
Testing its profundity
To its depths so dark and chill:—
And with so much freer will,
Must I have less liberty?
Streams are born, a coiled-up snake
When its path the streamlet finds,
Scarce a silver serpent winds
'Mong the flowers it must forsake,
But a song of praise doth wake,
Mournful though its music be,
To the plain that courteously
Opes a path through which it flies:—
And with life that never dies,

Must I have less liberty?
When I think of this I start,
Ætna-like in wild unrest
I would pluck from out my breast
Bit by bit my burning heart:—
For what law can so depart
From all right, as to deny
One lone man that liberty—
That sweet gift which God bestows
On the crystal stream that flows,
Birds and fish that float or fly?

ROSAURA: Fear and deepest sympathy
Do I feel at every word.

SIGISMUND: Who my sad lament has heard?
What! Clotaldo!

CLARIN: (*aside to his mistress*) Say 'tis he.

ROSAURA: No, 'tis but a wretch (ah, me!)
Who in these dark caves and cold
Hears the tale your lips unfold.

SIGISMUND: Then you'll die for listening so,
That you may not know I know
That you know the tale I told. (*Seizes her*)
Yes, you'll die for loitering near:
In these strong arms gaunt and grim
I will tear you limb from limb.

CLARIN: I am deaf and couldn't hear:—No!

ROSAURA: If human heart you bear,
'Tis enough that I prostrate me.
At thy feet, to liberate me!

SIGISMUND: Strange thy voice can so unbend me,
Strange thy sight can so suspend me,
And respect so penetrate me!
Who art thou? For though I see
Little from this lonely room,
This, my cradle and my tomb,
Being all the world to me,
And if birthday it could be,
Since my birthday I have known

## Life Is a Dream

But this desert wild and lone,
Where throughout my life's sad course
I have lived, a breathing corse,
I have moved, a skeleton;
And though I address or see
Never but one man alone,
Who my sorrows all hath known,
And through whom have come to me
Notions of earth, sky, and sea;
And though harrowing thee again,
Since thou'lt call me in this den,
Monster fit for bestial feasts,
I'm a man among wild beasts,
And a wild beast amongst men.
But though round me has been wrought
All this woe, from beasts I've learned
Polity, the same discerned
Heeding what the birds had taught,
And have measured in my thought
The fair orbits of the spheres;
You alone, 'midst doubts and fears,
Wake my wonder and surprise—
Give amazement to my eyes,
Admiration to my ears.
Every time your face I see
You produce a new amaze:
After the most steadfast gaze,
I again would gazer be.
I believe some hydropsy
Must affect my sight, I think
Death must hover on the brink
Of those wells of light, your eyes,
For I look with fresh surprise,
And though death result, I drink.
Let me see and die: forgive me;
For I do not know, in faith,
If to see you gives me death,
What to see you not would give me;

Something worse than death would grieve me,
Anger, rage, corroding care,
Death, but double death it were,
Death with tenfold terrors rife,
Since what gives the wretched life,
Gives the happy death, despair!

ROSAURA: Thee to see wakes such dismay,
Thee to hear I so admire,
That I'm powerless to inquire,
That I know not what to say:
Only this, that I to-day,
Guided by a wiser will,
Have here come to cure my ill,
Here consoled my grief to see,
If a wretch consoled can be
Seeing one more wretched still.
Of a sage, who roamed dejected,
Poor, and wretched, it is said,
That one day, his wants being fed
By the herbs which he collected,
"Is there one" (he thus reflected)
"Poorer than I am to-day?"
Turning round him to survey,
He his answer got, detecting
A still poorer sage collecting
Even the leaves he threw away.
Thus complaining to excess,
Mourning fate, my life I led,
And when thoughtlessly I said
To myself, "Does earth possess
One more steeped in wretchedness?"
I in thee the answer find.
Since revolving in my mind,
I perceive that all my pains
To become thy joyful gains
Thou hast gathered and entwined.
And if haply some slight solace
By these pains may be imparted,

## Life Is a Dream

Hear attentively the story
Of my life's supreme disasters.
I am. . . .

CLOTALDO: (*within*) Warders of this tower,
Who, or sleeping or faint-hearted,
Give an entrance to two persons
Who herein have burst a passage . . .

ROSAURA: New confusion now I suffer.

SIGISMUND: 'Tis Clotaldo, who here guards me,
Are not yet my miseries ended?

CLOTALDO: (*within*) Hasten hither, quick! be active!
And before they can defend them,
Kill them on the spot, or capture!
 (*Voices within*) Treason!

CLARIN: Watchguards of this tower,
Who politely let us pass here,
Since you have the choice of killing
Or of capturing, choose the latter.
 (*Enter* CLOTALDO *and* SOLDIERS; *he with a pistol, and all with their faces covered*)

CLOTALDO: (*aside to the* SOLDIERS) Keep your faces all well covered,
For it is a vital matter
That we should be known by no one,
While I question these two stragglers.

CLARIN: Are there masqueraders here?

CLOTALDO: Ye who in your ignorant rashness
Have passed through the bounds and limits
Of this interdicted valley,
'Gainst the edict of the King,
Who has publicly commanded
None should dare descry the wonder
That among these rocks is guarded,
Yield at once your arms and lives,
Or this pistol, this cold aspic
Formed of steel, the penetrating
Poison of two balls will scatter,

The report and fire of which
Will the air astound and startle.
SIGISMUND: Ere you wound them, ere you hurt them,
Will my life, O tyrant master,
Be the miserable victim
Of these wretched chains that clasp me;
Since in them, I vow to God,
I will tear myself to fragments
With my hands, and with my teeth,
In these rocks here, in these caverns,
Ere I yield to their misfortunes,
Or lament their sad disaster.
CLOTALDO: If you know that your misfortunes,
Sigismund, are unexampled,
Since before being born you died
By Heaven's mystical enactment;
If you know these fetters are
Of your furies oft so rampant
But the bridle that detains them,
But the circle that contracts them.
 (*To the* SOLDIERS) Why these idle boasts? The door
Of this narrow prison fasten;
Leave him there secured.
SIGISMUND: Ah, heavens,
It is wise of you to snatch me
Thus from freedom! since my rage
'Gainst you had become Titanic,
Since to break the glass and crystal
Gold-gates of the sun, my anger
On the firm-fixed rocks' foundations
Would have mountains piled of marble.
CLOTALDO: 'Tis that you should not so pile them
That perhaps these ills have happened.
 (*Some of the* SOLDIERS *lead* SIGISMUND *into his prison, th
 doors of which are closed upon him*)
ROSAURA: Since I now have seen how pride
Can offend thee, I were hardened
Sure in folly not here humbly

## Life Is a Dream

At thy feet for life to ask thee;
Then to me extend thy pity,
Since it were a special harshness
If humility and pride,
Both alike were disregarded.

CLARIN: If Humility and Pride
Those two figures who have acted
Many and many a thousand times
In the *autos sacramentales*,
Do not move you, I, who am neither
Proud nor humble, but a sandwich
Partly mixed of both, entreat you
To extend to us your pardon.

CLOTALDO: Ho!

SOLDIERS: My lord?

CLOTALDO: Disarm the two.
And their eyes securely bandage,
So that they may not be able
To see whither they are carried.

ROSAURA: This is, sir, my sword; to thee
Only would I wish to hand it,
Since in fine of all the others
Thou art chief, and I could hardly
Yield it unto one less noble.

CLARIN: Mine I'll give the greatest rascal
Of your troop: (*to a* SOLDIER) so take it, you.

ROSAURA: And if I must die, to thank thee
For thy pity, I would leave thee
This as pledge, which has its value
From the owner who once wore it;
That thou guard it well, I charge thee,
For although I do not know
What strange secret it may carry,
This I know, that some great mystery
Lies within this golden scabbard,
Since relying but on it
I to Poland here have traveled
To revenge a wrong.

**Clotaldo:** *(aside)* Just heavens!
What is this? Still graver, darker,
Grow my doubts and my confusion,
My anxieties and my anguish.—
Speak, who gave you this?

**Rosaura:** A woman.

**Clotaldo:** And her name?

**Rosaura:** To that my answer
Must be silence.

**Clotaldo:** But from what
Do you now infer, or fancy,
That this sword involves a secret?

**Rosaura:** She who gave it said: "Depart hence
Into Poland, and by study,
Stratagem, and skill so manage
That this sword may be inspected
By the nobles and the magnates
Of that land, for you, I know,
Will by one of them be guarded,"—
But his name, lest he was dead,
Was not then to me imparted.

**Clotaldo:** *(aside)* Bless me, Heaven! what's this I hear?
For so strangely has this happened,
That I cannot yet determine
If 'tis real or imagined.
This is the same sword that I
Left with beauteous Violante,
As a pledge unto its wearer,
Who might seek me out thereafter,
As a son that I would love him,
And protect him as a father.
What is to be done (ah, me!)
In confusion so entangled,
If he who for safety bore it
Bears it now but to dispatch him,
Since condemned to death he cometh
To my feet? How strange a marvel!
What a lamentable fortune!

## Life Is a Dream

How unstable! how unhappy!
This must be my son—the tokens
All declare it, superadded
To the flutter of the heart,
That to see him loudly rappeth
At the breast, and not being able
With its throbs to burst its chamber,
Does as one in prison, who,
Hearing tumult in the alley,
Strives to look from out the window;
Thus, not knowing what here passes
Save the noise, the heart uprusheth
To the eyes the cause to examine—
They the windows of the heart,
Out through which in tears it glances.
What is to be done? (O Heavens!)
What is to be done? To drag him
Now before the King were death;
But to hide him from my master,
That I cannot do, according
To my duty as a vassal.
Thus my loyalty and self-love
Upon either side attack me;
Each would win. But wherefore doubt?
Is not loyalty a grander,
Nobler thing than life, than honor?
Then let loyalty live, no matter
That he die; besides, he told me,
If I well recall his language,
That he came to revenge a wrong,
But a wronged man is a lazar,—
No, he cannot be my son,
Not the son of noble fathers.
But if some great chance, which no one
Can be free from, should have happened,
Since the delicate sense of honor
Is a thing so fine, so fragile,
That the slightest touch may break it,

Or the faintest breath may tarnish,
What could he do more, do more,
He whose cheek the blue blood mantles,
But at many risks to have come here
It again to reëstablish?
Yes, he is my son, my blood,
Since he shows himself so manly.
And thus then betwixt two doubts
A mid course alone is granted:
'Tis to seek the King, and tell him
Who he is, let what will happen.
A desire to save my honor
May appease my royal master;
Should he spare his life, I then
Will assist him in demanding
His revenge; but if the King
Should, persisting in his anger,
Give him death, then he will die
Without knowing I'm his father.—
Come, then, come then with me, strangers.

(*To* ROSAURA *and* CLARIN) Do not fear in your disaster
That you will not have companions
In misfortune; for so balanced
Are the gains of life or death,
That I know not which are larger.

(*Exeunt*)

(SCENE II. *A Hall in the Royal Palace*)

(*Enter at one side* ASTOLFO *and* SOLDIERS, *and at the other the* INFANTA ESTRELLA *and her* LADIES. *Military music and salutes within*)

ASTOLFO: Struck at once with admiration
At thy starry eyes outshining,
Mingle many a salutation,
Drums and trumpet-notes combining,
Founts and birds in alternation;

## Life Is a Dream

Wondering here to see thee pass,
Music in grand chorus gathers
All her notes from grove and grass:
Here are trumpets formed of feathers,
There are birds that breathe in brass.
All salute thee, fair Señora,
Ordnance as their Queen proclaim thee,
Beauteous birds as their Aurora,
As their Pallas trumpets name thee,
And the sweet flowers as their Flora;
For Aurora sure thou art,
Bright as day that conquers night—
Thine is Flora's peaceful part,
Thou art Pallas in thy might,
And as Queen thou rul'st my heart.

ESTRELLA: If the human voice obeying
Should with human action pair,
Then you have said ill in saying
All these flattering words and fair,
Since in truth they are gainsaying
This parade of victory,
'Gainst which I my standard rear,
Since they say, it seems to me,
Not the flatteries that I hear,
But the rigors that I see.
Think, too, what a base invention
From a wild beast's treachery sprung,—
Fraudful mother of dissension—
Is to flatter with the tongue,
And to kill with the intention.

ASTOLFO: Ill informed you must have been,
Fair Estrella, thus to throw
Doubt on my respectful mien:
Let your ear attentive lean
While the cause I strive show.
King Eustorgius the Fair,
Third so called, died, leaving two
Daughters, and Basilius heir;

Of his sisters I and you
Are the children—I forbear
To recall a single scene
Save what's needful. Clorilene,
Your good mother and my aunt,
Who is now a habitant
Of a sphere of sunnier sheen,
Was the elder, of whom you
Are the daughter; Recisunda,
Whom God guard a thousand years,
Her fair sister (Rosamunda
Were she called if names were true)
Wed in Muscovy, of whom
I was born. 'Tis needful now
The commencement to resume.
King Basilius, who doth bow
'Neath the weight of years, the doom
Age imposes, more inclined
To the studies of the mind
Than to women, wifeless, lone,
Without sons, to fill his throne
I and you our way would find.
You, the elder's child, averred,
That the crown you stood more nigh:
I, maintaining that you erred,
Held, though born of the younger, I,
Being a man, should be preferred.
Thus our mutual pretension
To our uncle we related,
Who replied that he would mention
Here, and on this day he stated,
What might settle the dissension.
With this end, from Muscovy
I set out, and with that view,
I to-day fair Poland see,
And not making war on you,
Wait till war you make on me.
Would to love—that God so wise—

## Life Is a Dream

That the crowd may be a sure
Astrologue to read the skies,
And this festive truce secure
Both to you and me the prize,
Making you a Queen, but Queen
By my will, our uncle leaving
You the throne we'll share between—
And my love a realm receiving
Dearer than a King's demesne.

ESTRELLA: Well, I must be generous too.
For a gallantry so fine;
This imperial realm you view,
If I wish it to be mine
'Tis to give it unto you.
Though if I the truth confessed,
I must fear your love may fail—
Flattering words are words at best,
For perhaps a truer tale
Tells that portrait on your breast.

ASTOLFO: On that point complete content
Will I give your mind, not here,
For each sounding instrument
 (*Drums are heard*)
Tells us that the King is near,
With his Court and Parliament.
 (*Enter the* KING BASILIUS, *with his retinue*)

ESTRELLA: Learned Euclid . . .
ASTOLFO: Thales wise . . .
ESTRELLA: The vast Zodiac . . .
ASTOLFO: The star spaces . . .
ESTRELLA: Who dost soar to . . .
ASTOLFO: Who dost rise . . .
ESTRELLA: The sun's orbit . . .
ASTOLFO: The stars' places . . .
ESTRELLA: To describe . . .
ASTOLFO: To map the skies . . .
ESTRELLA: Let me humbly interlacing . . .
ASTOLFO: Let me lovingly embracing . . .

ESTRELLA: Be the tendril of thy tree.
ASTOLFO: Bend respectfully my knee.
BASILIUS: Children, that dear word displacing
  Colder names, my arms here bless;
  And be sure, since you assented
  To my plan, my love's excess
  Will leave neither discontented,
  Or give either more or less.
  And though I from being old
  Slowly may the facts unfold,
  Hear in silence my narration,
  Keep reserved your admiration,
  Till the wondrous tale is told.
  You already know—I pray you
  Be attentive, dearest children,
  Great, illustrious Court of Poland,
  Faithful vassals, friends and kinsmen,
  You already know—my studies
  Have throughout the whole world given me
  The high title of "the learnéd,"
  Since 'gainst time and time's oblivion
  The rich pencils of Timanthes,
  The bright marbles of Lysippus,
  Universally proclaim me
  Through earth's bounds the great Basilius.
  You already know the sciences
  That I feel my mind most given to
  Are the subtle mathematics,
  By whose means my clear prevision
  Takes from rumor its slow office,
  Takes from time its jurisdiction
  Of, each day, new facts disclosing;
  Since in algebraic symbols
  When the fate of future ages
  On my tablets I see written,
  I anticipate time in telling
  What my science hath predicted.
  All those circles of pure snow,

## Life Is a Dream

All those canopies of crystal,
Which the sun with rays illumines,
Which the moon cuts in its circles,
All those orbs of twinkling diamond,
All those crystal globes that glisten,
All that azure field of stars
Where the zodiac signs are pictured,
Are the study of my life,
Are the books where heaven has written
Upon diamond-dotted paper,
Upon leaves by sapphires tinted,
With light luminous lines of gold,
In clear characters distinctly
All the events of human life,
Whether adverse or benignant.
These so rapidly I read
That I follow with the quickness
Of my thoughts the swiftest movements
Of their orbits and their circles.
Would to heaven, that ere my mind
To those mystic books addicted
Was the comment of their margins
And of all their leaves the index,
Would to heaven, I say, my life
Had been offered the first victim
Of its anger, that my death-stroke
Had in this way have been given me,
Since the unhappy find even merit
Is the fatal knife that kills them,
And his own self-murderer
Is the man whom knowledge injures!—
I may say so, but my story
So will say with more distinctness,
And to win your admiration
Once again I pray you listen.—
Clorilene, my wife, a son
Bore me, so by fate afflicted
That on his unhappy birthday

All Heaven's prodigies assisted.
Nay, ere yet to life's sweet light
Gave him forth her womb, that living
Sepulchre (for death and life
Have like ending and beginning),
Many a time his mother saw
In her dreams' delirious dimness
From her side a monster break,
Fashioned like a man, but sprinkled
With her blood, who gave her death,
By that human viper bitten.
Round his birthday came at last,
All its auguries fulfilling
(For the presages of evil
Seldom fail or even linger):
Came with such a horoscope,
That the sun rushed blood-red tinted
Into a terrific combat
With the dark moon that resisted;
Earth its mighty lists outspread
As with lessening lights diminished
Strove the twin-lamps of the sky.
'Tis of all the sun's eclipses
The most dreadful that it suffered
Since the hour its bloody visage
Wept the awful death of Christ.
For o'erwhelmed in glowing cinders
The great orb appeared to suffer
Nature's final paroxysm.
Gloom the glowing noontide darkened,
Earthquake shook the mightiest buildings,
Stones the angry clouds rained down,
And with blood ran red the rivers.
In this frenzy of the sun,
In its madness and delirium,
Sigismund was born, thus early
Giving proofs of his condition,
Since his birth his mother slew,

Just as if these words had killed her,
"I am a man, since good with evil
I repay here from the beginning,"—
I, applying to my studies,
Saw in them as 'twere forewritten
This, that Sigismund would be
The most cruel of all princes,
Of all men the most audacious,
Of all monarchs the most wicked;
That his kingdom through his means
Would be broken and partitioned,
The academy of the vices,
And the high school of sedition;
And that he himself, borne onward
By his crimes' wild course resistless,
Would even place his feet on me:
For I saw myself down-stricken,
Lying on the ground before him
(To say this what shame it gives me!)
While his feet on my white hairs
As a carpet were imprinted.
Who discredits threatened ill,
Specially an ill previsioned
By one's study, when self-love
Makes it his peculiar business?—
Thus then crediting the fates
Which far off my science witnessed,
All these fatal auguries
Seen though dimly in the distance,
I resolved to chain the monster
That unhappily life was given to,
To find out if yet the stars
Owned the wise man's weird dominion.
It was publicly proclaimed
That the sad ill-omened infant
Was stillborn. I then a tower
Caused by forethought to be builded
'Mid the rocks of these wild mountains

Where the sunlight scarce can gild it,
Its glad entrance being barred
By these rude shafts obeliscal.
All the laws of which you know,
All the edicts that prohibit
Any one on pain of death
That secluded part to visit
Of the mountain, were occasioned
By this cause, so long well hidden.
There still lives Prince Sigismund,
Miserable, poor, in prison.
Him alone Clotaldo sees,
Only tends to and speaks with him;
He the sciences has taught him,
He the Catholic religion
Has imparted to him, being
Of his miseries the sole witness.
Here there are three things: the first
I rate highest, since my wishes
Are, O Poland, thee to save
From the oppression, the affliction
Of a tyrant King, because
Of his country and his kingdom
He were no benignant father
Who to such a risk could give it.
Secondly, the thought occurs
That to take from mine own issue
The plain right that every law
Human and divine hath given him
Is not Christian charity;
For by no law am I bidden
To prevent another proving,
Say, a tyrant, or a villain,
To be one myself: supposing
Even my son should be so guilty,
That he should not crimes commit
I myself should first commit them.
Then the third and last point is,

## Life Is a Dream

That perhaps I erred in giving
Too implicit a belief
To the facts foreseen so dimly;
For although his inclination
Well might find its precipices,
He might possibly escape them:
For the fate the most fastidious,
For the impulse the most powerful,
Even the planets most malicious
Only make free will incline,
But can force not human wishes.
And thus 'twixt these different causes
Vacillating and unfixéd,
I a remedy have thought of
Which will with new wonder fill you.
I to-morrow morning purpose,
Without letting it be hinted
That he is my son, and therefore
Your true King, at once to fix him
As King Sigismund (for the name
Still he bears that first was given him)
'Neath my canopy, on my throne,
And in fine in my position,
There to govern and command you,
Where in dutiful submission
You will swear to him allegiance.
My resources thus are triple,
As the causes of disquiet
Were which I revealed this instant.
The first is; that he being prudent,
Careful, cautious, and benignant,
Falsifying the wild actions
That of him had been predicted,
You'll enjoy your natural prince,
He who has so long been living
Holding court amid these mountains,
With the wild beasts for his circle.
Then my next resource is this:

If he, daring, wild, and wicked,
Proudly runs with loosened rein
O'er the broad plain of the vicious,
I will have fulfilled the duty
Of my natural love and pity;
Then his righteous deposition
Will but prove my royal firmness,
Chastisement and not revenge
Leading him once more to prison.
My third course is this: the Prince
Being what my words have pictured,
From the love I owe you, vassals,
I will give you other princes
Worthier of the crown and scepter;
Namely, my two sisters' children,
Who their separate pretensions
Having happily commingled
By the holy bonds of marriage,
Will then fill their fit position.
This is what a king commands you,
This is what a father bids you,
This is what a sage entreats you,
This is what an old man wishes;
And as Seneca, the Spaniard,
Says, a king for all his riches
Is but slave of his Republic,
This is what a slave petitions.

ASTOLFO: If on me devolves the answer,
As being in this weighty business
The most interested party,
I, of all, express the opinion:—
Let Prince Sigismund appear;
He's thy son, that's all-sufficient.

ALL: Give to us our natural prince,
We proclaim him king this instant!

BASILIUS: Vassals, from my heart I thank you
For this deference to my wishes:—
Go, conduct to their apartments

# Life Is a Dream

These two columns of my kingdom,
On to-morrow you shall see him.

ALL: Live, long live great King Basilius!

(*Exeunt all, accompanying* ESTRELLA *and* ASTOLFO; *the King remains*)

(*Enter* CLOTALDO, ROSAURA, *and* CLARIN)

CLOTALDO: May I speak to you, Sire?

BASILIUS: Clotaldo,
You are always welcome with me.

CLOTALDO: Although coming to your feet
Shows how freely I'm admitted,
Still, Your Majesty, this once,
Fate as mournful as malicious
Takes from privilege its due right,
And from custom its permission.

BASILIUS: What has happened?

CLOTALDO: A misfortune,
Sire, which has my heart afflicted
At the moment when all joy
Should have overflown and filled it.

BASILIUS: Pray proceed.

CLOTALDO: This handsome youth here,
Inadvertently, or driven
By his daring, pierced the tower,
And the Prince discovered in it.
Nay. . . .

BASILIUS: Clotaldo, be not troubled
At this act, which if committed
At another time had grieved me,
But the secret so long hidden
Having myself told, his knowledge
Of the fact but matters little.
See me presently, for I
Much must speak upon this business,
And for me you much must do
For a part will be committed
To you in the strangest drama
That perhaps the world e'er witnessed.

As for these, that you may know
That I mean not your remissness
To chastise, I grant their pardon.
  (*Exit*)
CLOTALDO: Myriad years to my lord be given!
  (*Aside*) Heaven has sent a happier fate;
Since I need not now admit it,
I'll not say he is my son.—
Strangers who have wandered hither,
You are free.
ROSAURA: I give your feet
A thousand kisses.
CLARIN: I say misses,
For a letter more or less
'Twixt two friends is not considered.
ROSAURA: You have given me life, my lord,
And since by your act I'm living,
I eternally will own me
As your slave.
CLOTALDO: The life I've given
Is not really your true life,
For a man by birth uplifted
If he suffers an affront
Actually no longer liveth;
And supposing you have come here
For revenge as you have hinted,
I have not then given you life,
Since you have not brought it with you,
For no life disgraced is life.—
  (*Aside*) (This I say to arouse his spirit.)
ROSAURA: I confess I have it not,
Though by you it has been given me;
But revenge being wreaked, my honor
I will leave so pure and limpid,
All its perils overcome,
That my life may then with fitness
Seem to be a gift of yours.
CLOTALDO: Take this burnished sword which hither

You brought with you; for I know,
To revenge you, 'tis sufficient,
In your enemy's blood bathed red;
For a sword that once was girded
Round me (I say this the while
That to me it was committed),
Will know how to right you.
ROSAURA: Thus
In your name once more I gird it,
And on it my vengeance swear,
Though the enemy who afflicts me
Were more powerful.
CLOTALDO: Is he so?
ROSAURA: Yes; so powerful, I am hindered
Saying who he is, not doubting
Even for greater things your wisdom
And calm prudence, but through fear
Lest against me your prized pity
Might be turned.
CLOTALDO: 'Twill rather be,
By declaring it more kindled;
Otherwise you bar the passage
'Gainst your foe of my assistance.—
  (*Aside*) (Would that I but knew his name!)
ROSAURA: Not to think I set so little
Value on such confidence,
Know my enemy and my victim
Is no less than Prince Astolfo,
Duke of Muscovy.
CLOTALDO: (*aside*) Resistance
Badly can my grief supply
Since 'tis heavier than I figured.
Let us sift the matter deeper.—
If a Muscovite by birth, then
He who is your natural lord
Could not 'gainst you have committed
Any wrong; reseek your country,

    And abandon the wild impulse
That has driven you here.
ROSAURA: I know,
    Though a prince, he has committed
'Gainst me a great wrong.
CLOTALDO: He could not,
    Even although your face was stricken
By his angry hand. (*Aside*) (Oh, heavens!)
ROSAURA: Mine's a wrong more deep and bitter.
CLOTALDO: Tell it, then; it cannot be
    Worse than what my fancy pictures.
ROSAURA: I will tell it; though I know not,
    With the respect your presence gives me,
With the affection you awaken,
With the esteem your worth elicits,
How with bold face here to tell you
That this outer dress is simply
An enigma, since it is not
What it seems. And from this hint, then,
If I'm not what I appear,
And Astolfo with this princess
Comes to wed, judge how by him
I was wronged: I've said sufficient.
    (*Exeunt* ROSAURA *and* CLARIN)
CLOTALDO: Listen! hear me! wait! oh, stay!
    What a labyrinthine thicket
Is all this, where reason gives
Not a thread whereby to issue?
My own honor here is wronged,
Powerful is my foe's position,
I a vassal, she a woman;
Heaven reveal some way in pity,
Though I doubt it has the power;
When in such confused abysses,
Heaven is all one fearful presage,
And the world itself a riddle.
    (*Exit*)

# ACT II

(SCENE I. *A Hall in the Royal Palace*)

(*Enter* BASILIUS *and* CLOTALDO)

CLOTALDO: Everything has been effected
  As you ordered.
BASILIUS: How all happened
  Let me know, my good Clotaldo.
CLOTALDO: It was done, Sire, in this manner.
  With the tranquilizing draft,
  Which was made, as you commanded,
  Of confections duly mixed
  With some herbs, whose juice extracted
  Has a strange tyrannic power,
  Has some secret force imparted,
  Which all human sense and speech
  Robs, deprives, and counteracteth,
  And as 'twere a living corpse
  Leaves the man whose lips have quaffed it
  So asleep that all his senses,
  All his powers are overmastered. . . .
  —No need have we to discuss
  That this fact can really happen,
  Since, my lord, experience gives us
  Many a clear and proved example;
  Certain 'tis that Nature's secrets
  May by medicine be extracted,
  And that not an animal,
  Not a stone, or herb that's planted,
  But some special quality

Doth possess: for if the malice
Of man's heart, a thousand poisons
That give death, hath power to examine,
Is it then so great a wonder
That, their venom being abstracted,
If, as death by some is given,
Sleep by others is imparted?
Putting, then, aside the doubt
That 'tis possible this should happen,
A thing proved beyond all question
Both by reason and example . . .
—With the sleeping draft, in fine,
Made of opium superadded
To the poppy and the henbane,
I to Sigismund's apartment—
Cell, in fact—went down, and with him
Spoke awhile upon the grammar
Of the sciences, those first studies
Which mute Nature's gentle masters,
Silent skies and hills, had taught him;
In which school divine and ample,
The bird's song, the wild beast's roar,
Were a lesson and a language.
Then to raise his spirit more
To the high design you planned here,
I discoursed on, as my theme,
The swift flight, the stare undazzled
Of a pride-plumed eagle bold,
Which with back-averted talons,
Scorning the tame fields of air,
Seeks the sphere of fire, and passes
Through its flame a flash of feathers,
Or a comet's hair untangled.
I extolled its soaring flight,
Saying, "Thou at last art master
Of thy house, thou 'rt king of birds,
It is right thou should'st surpass them."
He who needed nothing more

Than to touch upon the matter
Of high royalty, with a bearing
As became him, boldly answered;
For in truth his princely blood
Moves, excites, inflames his ardor
To attempt great things: he said,
"In the restless realm of atoms
Given to birds, that even one
Should swear fealty as a vassal!
I, reflecting upon this,
Am consoled by my disasters,
For, at least, if I obey,
I obey through force: untrammeled,
Free to act, I ne'er will own
Any man on earth my master."—
This, his usual theme of grief,
Having roused him nigh to madness,
I occasion took to proffer
The drugged draft: he drank, but hardly
Had the liquor from the vessel
Passed into his breast, when fastest
Sleep his senses seized, a sweat,
Cold as ice, the life-blood hardened
In his veins, his limbs grew stiff,
So that, knew I not 'twas acted,
Death was there, feigned death, his life
I could doubt not had departed.
Then those, to whose care you trust
This experiment, in a carriage
Brought him here, where all things fitting
The high majesty and the grandeur
Of his person are provided.
In the bed of your state chamber
They have placed him, where the stupor
Having spent its force and vanished,
They, as 'twere yourself, my lord,
Him will serve as you commanded:
And if my obedient service

Seems to merit some slight largess,
I would ask but this alone
(My presumption you will pardon),
That you tell me, with what object
Have you, in this secret manner,
To your palace brought him here?

BASILIUS: Good Clotaldo, what you ask me
Is so just, to you alone
I would give full satisfaction.
Sigismund, my son, the hard
Influence of his hostile planet
(As you know) doth threat a thousand
Dreadful tragedies and disasters;
I desire to test if Heaven
(An impossible thing to happen)
Could have lied—if having given us
Proofs unnumbered, countless samples
Of his evil disposition,
He might prove more mild, more guarded
At the least, and self-subdued
By his prudence and true valor
Change his character; for 'tis man
That alone controls the planets.
This it is I wish to test,
Having brought him to this palace,
Where he'll learn he is my son,
And display his natural talents.
If he nobly hath subdued him,
He will reign; but if his manners
Show him tyrannous and cruel,
Then his chains once more shall clasp him.
But for this experiment,
Now you probably will ask me
Of what moment was't to bring him
Thus asleep and in this manner?
And I wish to satisfy you,
Giving all your doubts an answer.
If to-day he learns that he

## Life Is a Dream

Is my son, and some hours after
Finds himself once more restored
To his misery and his shackles,
Certain 'tis that from his temper
Blank despair may end in madness—
But once knowing who he is,
Can he be consoled thereafter?
Yes, and thus I wish to leave
One door open, one free passage,
By declaring all he saw
Was a dream. With this advantage
We attain two ends. The first
Is to put beyond all cavil
His condition, for on waking
He will show his thoughts, his fancies:
To console him is the second;
Since, although obeyed and flattered,
He beholds himself awhile,
And then back in prison shackled
Finds him, he will think he dreamed.
And he rightly so may fancy,
For, Clotaldo, in this world
All who live but dream they act here.

CLOTALDO: Reasons fail me not to show
That the experiment may not answer;
But there is no remedy now,
For a sign from the apartment
Tells me that he hath awoken
And even hitherward advances.

BASILIUS: It is best that I retire;
But do you, so long his master,
Near him stand; the wild confusions
That his waking sense may darken
Dissipate by simple truth.

CLOTALDO: Then your license you have granted
That I may declare it?

BASILIUS: Yes;
For it possibly may happen

That admonished of his danger
He may conquer his worst passions.
*(Exit)*
*(Enter* CLARIN*)*

CLARIN: *(aside)* Four good blows are all it cost me
To come here, inflicted smartly
By a red-robed halberdier,
With a beard to match his jacket.
At that price I see the show,
For no window's half so handy
As that which, without entreating
Tickets of the ticket-master,
A man carries with himself;
Since for all the feasts and galas
Cool effrontery is the window
Whence at ease he gazes at them.

CLOTALDO: *(aside)* This is Clarin, Heavens! of her,
Yes, I say, of her the valet,
She, who dealing in misfortunes,
Has my pain to Poland carried;—
Any news, friend Clarin?

CLARIN: News?
Yes, sir, since your great compassion
Is disposed Rosaura's outrage
To revenge, she has changed her habit,
And resumed her proper dress.

CLOTALDO: 'Tis quite right, lest possible scandal
Might arise.

CLARIN: More news: her name
Having changed and wisely bartered
For your niece's name, she now
So in honor has advanced her,
That among Estrella's ladies
She here with her in the palace
Lives.

CLOTALDO: 'Tis right that I once more
Should her honor reëstablish.

## Life Is a Dream

CLARIN: News; that anxiously she waiteth
For that very thing to happen,
When you may have time to try it.
CLOTALDO: Most discreetly has she acted;
Soon the time will come, believe me,
Happily to end this matter.
CLARIN: News, too; that she's well regaled,
Feasted like a queen, and flattered
On the strength of being your niece.
And the last news, and the saddest,
Is that I who here came with her
Am with hunger almost famished.
None remember me, or think
I am Clarin, clarion rather,
And that if that clarion sounded,
All the Court would know what passes.
For there are two things, to wit,
A brass clarion and a lackey,
That are bad at keeping secrets;
And it so may chance, if haply
I am forced to break my silence,
They of me may sing this passage:
"Never, when the day is near,
Does clarion sound more clear."
CLOTALDO: Your complaint is too well-founded;
I will get you satisfaction,
Meanwhile you may wait on me.
CLARIN: See, sir, Sigismund advances.

(*Music and song.* SIGISMUND *enters, lost in amazement. Servants minister to him, presenting costly robes.* CLOTALDO *and* CLARIN)

SIGISMUND: Help me, Heaven, what's this I see!
Help me, Heaven, what's this I view!
Things I scarce believe are true,
But, if true, which fright not me.
I in palaces of state?
I 'neath silks and cloth of gold?
I, around me, to behold

Rich-robed servants watch and wait?
I so soft a bed to press
While sweet sleep my senses bowed?
I to wake in such a crowd,
Who assist me even to dress?
'Twere deceit to say I dream,
Waking I recall my lot,
I am Sigismund, am I not?
Heaven make plain what dark doth seem!
Tell me, what has phantasy—
Wild, misleading, dream-adept—
So effected while I slept,
That I still the phantoms see?
But let that be as it may,
Why perplex myself and brood?
Better taste the present good,
Come what will some other day.

FIRST SERVANT: (*aside to the* SECOND SERVANT, *and to* CLARIN) What a sadness doth oppress him!
SECOND SERVANT: Who in such-like case would be
Less surprised and sad than he?
CLARIN: I for one.
SECOND SERVANT: (*to the* FIRST) You had best address him.
FIRST SERVANT: (*to* SIGISMUND) May they sing again?
SIGISMUND: No, no;
I don't care to hear them sing.
SECOND SERVANT: I conceived the song might bring
To your thought some ease.
SIGISMUND: Not so;
Voices that but charm the ear
Cannot soothe my sorrow's pain;
'Tis the soldier's martial strain
That alone I love to hear.
CLOTALDO: May Your Highness, mighty Prince,
Deign to let me kiss your hand,
I would first of all this land
My profound respect evince.
SIGISMUND: (*aside*) 'Tis my jailer! how can he

# Life Is a Dream

Change his harshness and neglect
To this language of respect?
What can have occurred to me?

CLOTALDO: The new state in which I find you
Must create a vague surprise,
Doubts unnumbered must arise
To bewilder and to blind you;
I would make your prospect fair,
Through the maze a path would show,
Thus, my lord, 'tis right you know
That you are the prince and heir
Of this Polish realm: if late
You lay hidden and concealed
'Twas that we were forced to yield
To the stern decrees of fate,
Which strange ills, I know not how,
Threatened on this land to bring
Should the laurel of a king
Ever crown thy princely brow.
Still relying on the power
Of your will the stars to bind,
For a man of resolute mind
Can them bind how dark they lower;
To this palace from your cell
In your lifelong turret keep
They have borne you while dull sleep
Held your spirit in its spell.
Soon to see you and embrace
Comes the King, your father, here—
He will make the rest all clear.

SIGISMUND: Why, thou traitor vile and base,
What need I to know the rest,
Since it is enough to know
Who I am my power to show,
And the pride that fills my breast?
Why this treason brought to light
Hast thou to thy country done,
As to hide from the King's son,

'Gainst all reason and all right,
This his rank?
CLOTALDO: Oh, destiny!
SIGISMUND: Thou the traitor's part hast played
'Gainst the law; the King betrayed,
And done cruel wrong to me;
Thus for each distinct offense
Have the law, the King, and I
Thee condemned this day to die
By my hands.
SECOND SERVANT: Prince...
SIGISMUND: No pretence
Shall undo the debt I owe you.
Caitiff, hence! By Heaven! I say,
If you dare to stop my way
From the window I will throw you.
SECOND SERVANT: Fly, Clotaldo!
CLOTALDO: Woe to thee,
In thy pride so powerful seeming,
Without knowing thou art dreaming!
  (*Exit*)
SECOND SERVANT: Think...
SIGISMUND: Away! don't trouble me.
SECOND SERVANT: He could not the King deny.
SIGISMUND: Bade to do a wrongful thing
He should have refused the King;
And, besides, his prince was I.
SECOND SERVANT: 'Twas not his affair to try
If the act was wrong or right.
SIGISMUND: You're indifferent, black or white,
Since so pertly you reply.
CLARIN: What the Prince says is quite true,
What you do is wrong, I say.
SECOND SERVANT: Who gave you this license, pray?
CLARIN: No one gave; I took it.
SIGISMUND: Who
Art thou, speak?
CLARIN: A meddling fellow,

## Life Is a Dream

Prating, prying, fond of scrapes,
General of all jackanapes,
And most merry when most mellow.

SIGISMUND: You alone in this new sphere
Have amused me.

CLARIN: That's quite true, sir,
For I am the great amuser
Of all Sigismunds who are here.
  (*Enter* ASTOLFO)

ASTOLFO: Thousand times be blest the day,
Prince, that gives thee to our sight,
Sun of Poland, whose glad light
Makes this whole horizon gay,
As when from the rosy fountains
Of the dawn the stream-rays run,
Since thou issuest like the sun
From the bosom of the mountains!
And though late do not defer
With thy sovereign light to shine;
Round thy brow the laurel twine—
Deathless crown.

SIGISMUND: God guard thee, sir.

ASTOLFO: In not knowing me I o'erlook,
But alone for this defect,
This response that lacks respect,
And due honor. Muscovy's Duke
Am I, and your cousin born,
Thus my equal I regard thee.

SIGISMUND: Did there, when I said "God guard thee,"
Lie concealed some latent scorn?—
Then if so, now having got
Thy big name, and seeing thee vexed,
When thou com'st to see me next
I will say God guard thee not.

SECOND SERVANT: (*to* ASTOLFO) Think, Your Highness, if he errs
Thus, his mountain birth's at fault,

Every word is an assault.
   (*To* SIGISMUND) Duke Astolfo, sir, prefers....
SIGISMUND: Tut! his talk became a bore,
   Nay his act was worse than that,
   He presumed to wear his hat.
SECOND SERVANT: As grandee.
SIGISMUND: But I am more.
SECOND SERVANT: Nevertheless respect should be
   Much more marked betwixt ye two
   Than 'twixt others.
SIGISMUND: And pray who
   Asked your meddling thus with me?
   (*Enter* ESTRELLA)
ESTRELLA: Welcome may Your Highness be,
   Welcomed oft to this thy throne,
   Which long longing for its own
   Finds at length its joy in thee;
   Where, in spite of bygone fears,
   May your reign be great and bright,
   And your life in its long flight
   Count by ages, not by years.
SIGISMUND: (*to* CLARIN) Tell me, thou, say, who can be
   This supreme of loveliness—
   Goddess in a woman's dress—
   At whose feet divine we see
   Heaven its choicest gifts doth lay?—
   This sweet maid? Her name declare.
CLARIN: 'Tis your star-named cousin fair.
SIGISMUND: Nay, the sun, 'twere best to say.—
   (*To* ESTRELLA) Though thy sweet felicitation
   Adds new splendor to my throne,
   'Tis for seeing thee alone
   That I merit gratulation;
   Therefore I a prize have drawn
   That I scarce deserved to win,
   And am doubly blessed therein:—
   Star, that in the rosy dawn
   Dimmest with transcendent ray

## Life Is a Dream

Orbs that brightest gem the blue,
What is left the sun to do,
When thou risest with the day?—
Give me then thy hand to kiss,
In whose cup of snowy whiteness
Drinks the day delicious brightness.

ESTRELLA: What a courtly speech is this?

ASTOLFO: (*aside*) If he takes her hand I feel
I am lost.

SECOND SERVANT: (*aside*) Astolfo's grief
I perceive, and bring relief:—
Think, my lord, excuse my zeal,
That perhaps this is too free,
Since Astolfo . . .

SIGISMUND: Did I say
Woe to him that stops my way?—

SECOND SERVANT: What I said was just.

SIGISMUND: To me
This is tiresome and absurd.
Nought is just, or good or ill,
In my sight that balks my will.

SECOND SERVANT: Why, my lord, yourself I heard
Say in any righteous thing
It was proper to obey.

SIGISMUND: You must, too, have heard me say
Him I would from window throw
Who should tease me or defy?

SECOND SERVANT: Men like me perhaps might show
That could not be done, sir.

SIGISMUND: No?
Then, by Heaven, at least, I'll try!
(*He seizes him in his arms and rushes to the side. All follow, and return immediately*)

ASTOLFO: What is this I see? Oh, woe!

ESTRELLA: Oh, prevent him! Follow me!
(*Exit*)

SIGISMUND: (*returning*) From the window into the sea
He has fallen; I told him so.

ASTOLFO: These strange bursts of savage malice
  You should regulate, if you can;
  Wild beasts are to civilized man
  As rude mountains to a palace.
SIGISMUND: Take a bit of advice for that:
  Pause ere such bold words are said,
  Lest you may not have a head
  Upon which to hang your hat.
    (*Exit* ASTOLFO)
    (*Enter* BASILIUS)
BASILIUS: What's all this?
SIGISMUND: A trifling thing:
  One who teased and thwarted me
  I have just thrown into the sea.
CLARIN: (*to* SIGISMUND) Know, my lord, it is the King.
BASILIUS: Ere the first day's sun hath set,
  Has thy coming cost a life?
SIGISMUND: Why he dared me to the strife,
  And I only won the bet.
BASILIUS: Prince, my grief, indeed is great,
  Coming here when I had thought
  That admonished thou wert taught
  To o'ercome the stars and fate,
  Still to see such rage abide
  In the heart I hoped was free,
  That thy first sad act should be
  A most fearful homicide.
  How could I by love conducted,
  Trust me to thine arms' embracing,
  When their haughty interlacing,
  Has already been instructed
  How to kill? For who could see,
  Say, some dagger bare and bloody,
  By some wretch's heart made ruddy,
  But would fear it? Who is he,
  Who may happen to behold
  On the ground the gory stain
  Where another man was slain

## Life Is a Dream

But must shudder? The most bold
Yields at once to Nature's laws;
Thus I, seeing in your arms
The dread weapon that alarms,
And the stain, must fain withdraw;
And though in embraces dear
I would press you to my heart,
I without them must depart,
For, alas! your arms I fear.

SIGISMUND: Well, without them I must stay,
As I've stayed for many a year,
For a father so severe,
Who could treat me in this way,
Whose unfeeling heart could tear me
From his side even when a child,
Who, a denizen of the wild,
As a monster there could rear me,
And by many an artful plan
Sought my death, it cannot grieve me
Much his arms will not receive me
Who has scarcely left me man.

BASILIUS: Would to God it had not been
Act of mine that name conferred,
Then thy voice I ne'er had heard,
Then thy boldness ne'er had seen.

SIGISMUND: Did you manhood's right retain,
I would then have nought to say,
But to give and take away
Gives me reason to complain;
For although to give with grace
Is the noblest act 'mongst men,
To take back the gift again
In the basest of the base.

BASILIUS: This then is thy grateful mood
For my changing thy sad lot
To a prince's!

SIGISMUND: And for what
Should I show my gratitude!

Tyrant of my will o'erthrown,
If thou hoary art and gray,
Dying, what dost give me? Say,
Dost thou give what's not mine own?
Thou'rt my father and my King,
Then the pomp these walls present
Comes to me by due descent
As a simple, natural thing.
Yes, this sunshine pleaseth me,
But 'tis not through thee I bask;
Nay, a reckoning I might ask
For the life, love, liberty
That through thee I've lost so long:
Thine 'tis rather to thank me,
That I do not claim from thee
Compensation for my wrong.

BASILIUS: Still untamed and uncontrolled;—
Heaven fulfills its word I feel,
I to that same court appeal
'Gainst thy taunts, thou vain and bold,
But although the truth thou'st heard,
And now know'st thy name and race,
And dost see thee in this place,
Where to all thou art preferred,
Yet be warned, and on thee take
Ways more mild and more beseeming,
For perhaps thou art but dreaming,
When it seems that thou'rt awake.
 (*Exit*)

SIGISMUND: Is this, then, a phantom scene?—
Do I wake in seeming show?—
No, I dream not, since I know
What I am and what I've been.
And although thou should'st repent thee,
Remedy is now too late.
Who I am I know, and fate,
Howsoe'er thou should'st lament thee,
Cannot take from me my right

## Life Is a Dream

Of being born this kingdom's heir.
If I saw myself erewhile
Prisoned, bound, kept out of sight,
'Twas that never on my mind
Dawned the truth; but now I know
Who I am—a mingled show
Of the man and beast combined.

(*Enter* ROSAURA, *in female attire*)

ROSAURA: (*aside*) To wait upon Estrella I come here,
And lest I meet Astolfo tremble with much fear;
Clotaldo's wishes are
The Duke should know me not, and from afar
See me, if see he must.
My honor is at stake, he says; my trust
Is in Clotaldo's truth.
He will protect my honor and my youth.

CLARIN: (*to* SIGISMUND) Of all this palace here can boast,
All that you yet have seen, say which has pleased you most?

SIGISMUND: Nothing surprised me, nothing scared,
Because for everything I was prepared;
But if I felt for aught, or more or less
Of admiration, 'twas the loveliness
Of woman; I have read
Somewhere in books on which my spirit fed,
That which caused God the greatest care to plan,
Because in him a little world he formed was man;
But this were truer said, unless I err,
Of woman, for a little heaven he made in her;
She who in beauty from her birth
Surpasses man as heaven surpasseth earth;
Nay, more, the one I see.

ROSAURA: (*aside*) The Prince is here; I must this instant flee.

SIGISMUND: Hear, woman! stay;
Nor wed the western with the orient ray,
Flying with rapid tread;
For joined the orient rose and western red,
The light and the cold gloom,

The day will sink untimely to its tomb.
But who is this I see?
ROSAURA: (*aside*) I doubt and yet believe that it is he.
SIGISMUND: (*aside*) This beauty I have seen
Some other time.
ROSAURA: (*aside*) This proud, majestic mien,
This form I once saw bound
Within a narrow cell.
SIGISMUND: (*aside*) My life I have found.—
(*Aloud*) Woman, the sweetest name
That man can breathe, or flattering language frame,
Who art thou? for before
I see thee, I believe and I adore;
Faith makes my love sublime,
Persuading me we've met some other time.
Fair woman, speak; my will must be obeyed.
ROSAURA: In bright Estrella's train a hapless maid.—
(*Aside*) He must not know my name.
SIGISMUND: The sun, say rather, of that star whose flame,
However bright its blaze
Is but the pale reflection of thy rays.
In the fair land of flowers,
The realm of sweets that lies in odorous bowers,
The goddess rose I have seen
By right divine of beauty reign as queen.
I have seen where brightest shine
Gems, the assembled glories of the mine,
The brilliant throng elect the diamond king
For the superior splendor it doth fling.
Amid the halls of light,
Where the unresting star-crowds meet at night,
I have seen fair Hesper rise
And take the foremost place of all the skies.
And in that higher zone
Where the sun calls the planets round his throne,
I have seen, with sovereign sway,
That he presides the oracle of the day.
How, then, 'mid flowers of earth or stars of air,

# Life Is a Dream

Mid stones or suns, if that which is most fair
The preference gains, canst thou
Before a lesser beauty bend and bow,
When thine own charms compose
Something more bright than sun, stone, star, or rose?
   (*Enter* CLOTALDO)

CLOTALDO: (*aside*) To calm Prince Sigismund devolves on me,
Because 'twas I who reared him:—What do I see?

ROSAURA: Thy favor, sir, I prize;
To thee the silence of my speech replies;
For when the reason's dull, the mind depressed,
He best doth speak who keeps his silence best.

SIGISMUND: You must not leave me. Stay.
What! would you rob my senses of the ray
Your beauteous presence gave?

ROSAURA: That license, from your Highness, I must crave.

SIGISMUND: The violent efforts that you make
Show that you do not ask the leave you take.

ROSAURA: I hope to take it, if it is not given.

SIGISMUND: You rouse my courtesy to rage, by Heaven!—
In me resistance, as it were, distils
A cruel poison that my patience kills.

ROSAURA: Then though that poison may be strong,
The source of fury, violence, and wrong,
Potent thy patience to subdue,
It dare not the respect to me that's due.

SIGISMUND: As if to show I may,
You take the terror of your charms away.
For I am but too prone
To attempt the impossible; I to-day have thrown
Out of this window one who said, like you,
I dare not do the thing I said I would do.
Now just to show I can,
I may throw out your honor, as the man.

CLOTALDO: (*aside*) More obstinate doth he grow;
What course to take, O Heavens! I do not know,
When wild desire, nay, crime,
Perils my honor for the second time.

ROSAURA: Not vainly, as I see,
  This hapless land was warned thy tyranny
  In fearful scandals would eventuate,
  In wrath and wrong, in treachery, rage and hate.
  But who in truth could claim
  Aught from a man who is but a man in name,
  Audacious, cruel, cold,
  Inhuman, proud, tyrannical and bold,
  'Mong beasts a wild beast born?—
SIGISMUND: It was to save me from such words of scorn
  So courteously I spoke,
  Thinking to bind you by a gentler yoke;
  But if I am in aught what you have said,
  Then, as God lives, I will be all you dread.
  Ho, there! here leave us. See to it at your cost,
  The door be locked; let no one in.
     (*Exeunt* CLARIN *and the attendants*)
ROSAURA: I'm lost!
  Consider . . .
SIGISMUND: I'm a despot, and 'tis vain
  You strive to move me, or my will restrain.
CLOTALDO: (*aside*) Oh, what a moment! what an agony!
  I will go forth and stop him though I die.
     (*He advances*)
  My lord, consider, stay . . .
SIGISMUND: A second time you dare to cross my way,
  Old dotard; do you hold
  My rage in such slight awe you are so bold?
  What brought you hither? Speak!
CLOTALDO: The accents of this voice, however weak,
  To tell you to restrain
  Your passions, if as King you wish to reign,—
  Not to be cruel, though you deem
  Yourself the lord of all, for all may be a dream.
SIGISMUND: You but provoke my rage
  By these old saws, the unwelcome light of age,
  In killing you, at least I'll see
  If 'tis a dream or truth.

# Life Is a Dream

*(As he is about to draw his dagger* CLOTALDO *detains it, and throws himself on his knees)*

CLOTALDO: Sole hope for me
To save my life is thus to humbly kneel.

SIGISMUND: Take your audacious hand from off my steel.

CLOTALDO: Till some kind aid be sent,
Till some one come who may your rage prevent,
I will not loose my hold.

ROSAURA: Oh, Heaven!

SIGISMUND: I say,
Loose it, old dotard, grim and gaunt and gray,
Or by another death
*(They struggle)*
I'll crush you in my arms while you have breath.

ROSAURA: Quick! quick! they slay
Clotaldo, help! oh, help!
*(Exit)*
*(*ASTOLFO *enters at this moment, and* CLOTALDO *falls at his feet; he stands between them)*

ASTOLFO: This strange affray,
What can it mean, magnanimous Prince? would you
So bright a blade imbrue
In blood that age already doth congeal?
Back to its sheath return the shining steel.

SIGISMUND: Yes, when it is bathed red
In his base blood.

ASTOLFO: This threatened life hath fled
For sanctuary to my feet;
I must protect it in that poor retreat.

SIGISMUND: Protect your own life, then, for in this way,
Striking at it, I will the grudge repay
I owe you for the past.

ASTOLFO: I thus defend
My life; but majesty will not offend.
*(*ASTOLFO *draws his sword and they fight)*

CLOTALDO: Oh! wound him not, my lord.
*(Enter* BASILIUS, ESTRELLA *and Attendants)*

BASILIUS: Swords flashing here!—

ESTRELLA: *(aside)* Astolfo is engaged:—Oh, pain severe!
BASILIUS: What caused this quarrel? Speak, say why?
ASTOLFO: 'Tis nothing now, my lord, since thou art by.
SIGISMUND: 'Tis much, although thou now art by, my lord.
   I wished to kill this old man with my sword.
BASILIUS: Did you not then respect
   These snow-white hairs?
CLOTALDO: My lord will recollect
   They scarce deserved it, being mine.
SIGISMUND: Who dares
   To ask of me do I respect white hairs?
   Your own some day
   My feet may trample in the public way,
   For I have not as yet revenged my wrong,
   Your treatment so unjust and my sad state so long.
     (*Exit*)
BASILIUS: But ere that dawn doth break,
   You must return to sleep, where when you wake
   All that hath happened here will seem—
   As is the glory of the world—a dream.
     (*Exeunt the King,* CLOTALDO, *and Attendants*)
ASTOLFO: Ah, how rarely fate doth lie
   When it some misfortune threatens!
   Dubious when 'tis good that's promised,
   When 'tis evil, ah, too certain!—
   What a good astrologer
   Would he be, whose art foretelleth
   Only cruel things; for, doubtless,
   They would turn out true forever!
   This in Sigismund and me
   Is exemplified, Estrella,
   Since between our separate fortunes
   Such a difference is presented.
   In his case had been foreseen
   Murders, miseries, and excesses,
   And in all they turned out true,
   Since all happened as expected.
   But in mine, here seeing, lady,

# Life Is a Dream

Rays so rare and so resplendent
That the sun is but their shadow.
And even heaven a faint resemblance,
When fate promised me good fortune,
Trophies, praises, and all blessings,
It spoke ill and it spoke well;
For it was of both oppressive,
When it held out hopes of favor,
But disdain alone effected.

ESTRELLA: Oh, I doubt not these fine speeches
Are quite true, although intended
Doubtless for that other lady,
She whose portrait was suspended
From your neck, when first, Astolfo,
At this Court here you addressed me.
This being so, 'tis she alone
Who these compliments deserveth.
Go and pay them to herself,
For like bills that are protested
In the counting-house of love,
Are those flatteries and finesses
Which to other kings and ladies
Have been previously presented.

(*Enter* ROSAURA)

ROSAURA: (*aside*) Well, thank God, my miseries
Have attained their lowest level,
Since by her who sees this sight
Nothing worse can be expected.

ASTOLFO: Then that portrait from my breast
Shall be taken, that thy perfect
Beauty there may reign instead.
For where bright Estrella enters
Shadow cannot be, or star
Where the sun; I go to fetch it.—
(*Aside*) Pardon, beautiful Rosaura,
This offense; the absent never,
Man or woman, as this shows,

Faith or plighted vows remember.
*(Exit)*
(ROSAURA *comes forward*)

ROSAURA: *(aside)* Not a single word I heard,
Being afraid they might observe me.

ESTRELLA: Oh, Astrea!

ROSAURA: My good lady!

ESTRELLA: Nothing could have pleased me better
Than your timely coming here.
I have something confidential
To entrust you with.

ROSAURA: You honor
Far too much my humble service.

ESTRELLA: Brief as is the time, Astrea,
I have known you, you already
Of my heart possess the keys.
'Tis for this and your own merits
That I venture to entrust you
With what oft I have attempted
From myself to hide.

ROSAURA: Your slave!

ESTRELLA: Then concisely to express it,
Know, Astolfo, my first cousin
('Tis enough that word to mention,
For some things may best be said
When not spoken but suggested),
Soon expects to wed with me,
If my fate so far relenteth,
As that by one single bliss
All past sorrows may be lessened.
I was troubled, the first day
That we met, to see suspended
From his neck a lady's portrait.
On the point I urged him gently,
He so courteous and polite
Went immediately to get it,
And will bring it here. From him
I should feel quite disconcerted

## Life Is a Dream

To receive it. You here stay,
And request him to present it
Unto you. I say no more.
You are beautiful and clever,
You must know too what is love.
   (*Exit*)

ROSAURA: Would I knew it not! O help me
Now, kind Heaven! for who could be
So prudential, so collected,
As to know how best to act
In so painful a dilemma?
Is there in the world a being,
Is there one a more inclement
Heaven has marked with more misfortunes,
Has 'mid more of sorrow centered?—
What, bewildered, shall I do,
When 'tis vain to be expected
That my reason can console me,
Or consoling be my helper?
From my earliest misfortune
Everything that I've attempted
Has been but one misery more—
Each the other's sad successor,
All inheritors of themselves.
Thus, the Phœnix they resemble,
One is from the other born,
New life springs where old life endeth,
And the young are warmly cradled
By the ashes of the elder.
Once a wise man called them cowards,
Seeing that misfortunes never
Have been seen to come alone.
But I call them brave, intrepid,
Who go straight unto their end,
And ne'er turn their backs in terror:—
By the man who brings them with him
Everything may be attempted,
Since he need on no occasion

Have the fear of being deserted.
I may say so, since at all times,
Whatsoever life presented,
I, without them, never saw me,
Nor will they grow weary ever,
Till they see me in death's arms,
Wounded by fate's final weapon.
Woe is me! but what to-day
Shall I do in this emergence?—
If I tell my name, Clotaldo,
Unto whom I am indebted
For my very life and honor,
May be with me much offended;
Since he said my reparation
Must in silence be expected.
If I tell not to Astolfo
Who I am, and he detects me
How can I dissemble then?
For although a feigned resemblance
Eyes and voice and tongue might try,
Ah, the truthful heart would tremble,
And expose the lie. But wherefore
Study what to do? 'Tis certain
That however I may study,
Think beforehand how to nerve me,
When at last the occasion comes,
Then alone what grief suggesteth
I will do, for no one holds
In his power the heart's distresses.
And thus what to say or do
As my soul cannot determine,
Grief must only reach to-day
Its last limit, pain be ended,
And at last an exit make
From the doubts that so perplex me
How to act: but until then
Help me, Heaven, oh, deign to help me!

## Life Is a Dream

(*Enter* Astolfo, *with the portrait*)

ASTOLFO: Here then is the portrait, Princess:
But, good God!

ROSAURA: Your Highness trembles;
What has startled, what surprised you?

ASTOLFO: Thee, Rosaura, to see present.

ROSAURA: I Rosaura? Oh, Your Highness
Is deceived by some resemblance
Doubtless to some other lady;
I'm Astrea, one who merits
Not the glory of producing
An emotion so excessive.

ASTOLFO: Ah, Rosaura, thou mayst feign,
But the soul bears no deception,
And though seeing thee as Astrea,
As Rosaura it must serve thee.

ROSAURA: I, not knowing what Your Highness
Speaks of, am of course prevented
From replying aught but this,
That Estrella (the bright Hesper
Of this sphere) was pleased to order
That I here should wait expectant
For that portrait, which to me
She desires you give at present:
For some reason she prefers
It through me should be presented—
So Estrella—say, my star—
Wishes—so a fate relentless
Wills—in things that bring me loss—
So Estrella now expecteth.

ASTOLFO: Though such efforts you attempt,
Still how badly you dissemble,
My Rosaura! Tell the eyes
In their music to keep better
Concert with the voice, because
Any instrument whatever
Would be out of tune that sought
To combine and blend together

  The true feelings of the heart
  With the false words speech expresses.
ROSAURA: I wait only, as I said,
  For the portrait.
ASTOLFO: Since you're bent then
  To the end to keep this tone,
  I adopt it, and dissemble.
  Tell the Princess, then, Astrea,
  That I so esteem her message,
  That to send to her a copy
  Seems to me so slight a present,
  How so highly it is valued
  By myself, I think it better
  To present the original,
  And you easily may present it,
  Since, in point of fact, you bring it
  With you in your own sweet person.
ROSAURA: When it has been undertaken
  By a man, bold, brave, determined,
  To obtain a certain object,
  Though he get perhaps a better,
  Still not bringing back the first
  He returns despised: I beg, then,
  That Your Highness give the portrait;
  I, without it, dare not venture.
ASTOLFO: How, then, if I do not give it
  Will you get it?
ROSAURA: I will get it
  Thus, ungrateful.
   (*She attempts to snatch it*)
ASTOLFO: 'Tis in vain.
ROSAURA: It must ne'er be seen, no, never
  In another woman's hands.
ASTOLFO: Thou art dreadful.
ROSAURA: Thou deceptive.
ASTOLFO: Oh, enough, Rosaura mine.
ROSAURA: Thine! Thou liest, base deserter.

# Life Is a Dream

*(Both struggle for the portrait)*
*(Enter ESTRELLA)*

ESTRELLA: Prince! Astrea! What is this?
ASTOLFO: *(aside)* Heavens! Estrella!
ROSAURA: *(aside)* Love befriend me;
  Give me wit enough my portrait
  To regain:—*(To ESTRELLA)* If thou would'st learn then
  What the matter is, my lady,
  I will tell thee.
ASTOLFO: *(aside to ROSAURA)* Would'st o'erwhelm me?
ROSAURA: You commanded me to wait here
  For the Prince, and, representing
  You, to get from him a portrait.
  I remained alone, expecting,
  And, as often by one thought
  Is some other thought suggested,
  Seeing that you spoke of portraits,
  I, reminded thus, remembered
  That I had one of myself
  In my sleeve: I wished to inspect it,
  For a person quite alone
  Even by trifles is diverted.
  From my hand I let it fall
  On the ground; the Prince, who entered
  With the other lady's portrait,
  Raised up mine, but so rebellious
  Was he to what you had asked him
  That, instead of his presenting
  One, he wished to keep the other.
  Since he mine will not surrender
  To my prayers and my entreaties:
  Angry at this ill-timed jesting
  I endeavored to regain it,
  That which in his hand is held there
  Is my portrait, if you see it;
  You can judge of the resemblance.
ESTRELLA: Duke, at once, give up the portrait.
  *(She takes it from his hand)*

ASTOLFO: Princess . . .
ESTRELLA: Well, the tints were blended
  By no cruel hand, methinks.
ROSAURA: Is it like me?
ESTRELLA: Like! 'Tis perfect.
ROSAURA: Now demand from him the other.
ESTRELLA: Take your own, and leave our presence.
ROSAURA: (*aside*) I have got my portrait back;
  Come what may I am contented.
    (*Exit*)
ESTRELLA: Give me now the other portrait;
  For—although perhaps I never
  May again address or see you—
  I desire not, no, to let it
  In your hands remain, if only
  For my folly in requesting
  You to give it.
ASTOLFO: (*aside*) How escape
  From this singular dilemma?—
  Though I wish, most beauteous Princess,
  To obey thee and to serve thee,
  Still I cannot give the portrait
  Thou dost ask for, since . . .
ESTRELLA: A wretched
  And false-hearted lover art thou.
  Now I wish it not presented,
  So to give thee no pretext
  For reminding me that ever
  I had asked it at thy hands.
    (*Exit*)
ASTOLFO: Hear me! listen! wait! remember!—
  God, what hast thou done, Rosaura?
  Why, or wherefore, on what errand,
  To destroy thyself and me
  Hast thou Poland rashly entered?
    (*Exit*)

## Life Is a Dream

(SCENE II. *Prison of the Prince in the Tower*)

(SIGISMUND, *as at the commencement, clothed in skins, chained, and lying on the ground;* CLOTALDO, *two* SERVANTS, *and* CLARIN)

CLOTALDO: Leave him here on the ground,
  Where his day,—its pride being o'er,—
  Finds its end too.
A SERVANT: As before
  With the chain his feet are bound.
CLARIN: Never from that sleep profound
  Wake, O Sigismund, or rise,
  To behold with wondering eyes
  All thy glorious life o'erthrown,
  Like a shadow that hath flown,
  Like a bright brief flame that dies!
CLOTALDO: One who can so wisely make
  Such reflections on this case
  Should have ample time and space,
  Even for the Solon's sake,
  To discuss it; (*to the* SERVANT) him you'll take
  To this cell here, and keep bound.
    (*Pointing to an adjoining room*)
CLARIN: But why me?
CLOTALDO: Because 'tis found
  Safe, when clarions secrets know,
  Clarions to lock up, that so
  They may not have power to sound.
CLARIN: Did I, since you treat me thus,
  Try to kill my father? No.
  Did I from the window throw
  That unlucky Icarus?
  Is my drink somniferous?
  Do I dream? Then why be pent?
CLOTALDO: 'Tis a clarion's punishment.
CLARIN: Then a horn of low degree,
  Yea, a cornet I will be,
  A safe, silent instrument.

*(They take him away, and* CLOTALDO *remains alone)*
*(Enter* BASILIUS, *disguised)*

BASILIUS: Hark, Clotaldo!
CLOTALDO: My lord here?
  Thus disguised, Your Majesty?
BASILIUS: Foolish curiosity
  Leads me in this lowly gear
  To find out, ah, me! with fear,
  How the sudden change he bore.
CLOTALDO: There behold him as before
  In his miserable state.
BASILIUS: Wretched Prince! unhappy fate!
  Birth by baneful stars watched o'er!—
  Go and wake him cautiously,
  Now that strength and force lie chained
  By the opiate he hath drained.
CLOTALDO: Muttering something restlessly,
  See he lies.
BASILIUS: Let's listen; he
  May some few clear words repeat.
SIGISMUND: *(speaking in his sleep)* Perfect Prince is he whose heat
  Smites the tyrant where he stands,
  Yes, Clotaldo dies by my hands,
  Yes, my sire shall kiss my feet.
CLOTALDO: Death he threatens in his rage.
BASILIUS: Outrage vile he doth intend.
CLOTALDO: He my life has sworn to end.
BASILIUS: He has vowed to insult my age.
SIGISMUND: *(still sleeping)* On the mighty world's great stage,
  'Mid the admiring nations' cheer,
  Valor mine, that has no peer,
  Enter thou: the slave so shunned
  Now shall reign Prince Sigismund,
  And his sire his wrath shall fear.—
    *(He awakes)*
  But, ah me! Where am I? Oh!—

# Life Is a Dream

**BASILIUS:** Me I must not let him see.
   (*To* CLOTALDO) Listening I close by will be,
What you have to do you know.
   (*He retires*)

**SIGISMUND:** Can it possibly be so?
  Is the truth not what it seemed?
  Am I chained and unredeemed?
  Art not thou my lifelong tomb,
  Dark old tower? Yes! What a doom!
  God! what wondrous things I've dreamed!

**CLOTALDO:** Now in this delusive play
  Must my special part be taken:—
  Is it not full time to waken?

**SIGISMUND:** Yes, to waken well it may.

**CLOTALDO:** Wilt thou sleep the livelong day?—
  Since we gazing from below
  Saw the eagle sailing slow,
  Soaring through the azure sphere,
  All the time thou waited here,
  Didst thou never waken?

**SIGISMUND:** No,
  Nor even now am I awake,
  Since such thoughts my memory fill,
  That it seems I'm dreaming still:
  Nor is this a great mistake;
  Since if dreams could phantoms make
  Things of actual substance seen,
  I things seen may phantoms deem.
  Thus a double harvest reaping,
  I can see when I am sleeping,
  And when waking I can dream.

**CLOTALDO:** What you may have dreamed of, say.

**SIGISMUND:** If I thought it only seemed,
  I would tell not what I dreamed,
  But what I behold, I may.
  I awoke, and lo! I lay
  (Cruel and delusive thing!)
  In a bed whose covering,

Bright with blooms from rosy bowers,
Seemed a tapestry of flowers
Woven by the hand of Spring.
Then a crowd of nobles came,
Who addressed me by the name
Of their prince, presenting me
Gems and robes, on bended knee.
Calm soon left me, and my frame
Thrilled with joy to hear thee tell
Of the fate that me befell,
For though now in this dark den,
I was Prince of Poland then.

CLOTALDO: Doubtless you repaid me well?
SIGISMUND: No, not well: for, calling thee
Traitor vile, in furious strife
Twice I strove to take thy life.
CLOTALDO: But why all this rage 'gainst me?
SIGISMUND: I was master, and would be
Well revenged on foe and friend.
Love one woman could defend . . .
That, at least, for truth I deem,
All else ended like a dream,
*That* alone can never end.
    (*The King withdraws*)
CLOTALDO: (*aside*) From his place the King hath gone,
Touched by his pathetic words:—
    (*Aloud*) Speaking of the king of birds
Soaring to ascend his throne,
Thou didst fancy one thine own;
But in dreams, however bright,
Thou shouldst still have kept in sight
How for years I tended thee,
For 'twere well, whoe'er we be,
Even in dreams to do what's right.
    (*Exit*)
SIGISMUND: That is true: then let's restrain
This wild rage, this fierce condition
Of the mind, this proud ambition,

## Life Is a Dream

Should we ever dream again:
And we'll do so, since 'tis plain,
In this world's uncertain gleam,
That to live is but to dream:
Man dreams what he is, and wakes
Only when upon him breaks
Death's mysterious morning beam.
The king dreams he is a king,
And in this delusive way
Lives and rules with sovereign sway;
All the cheers that round him ring,
Born of air, on air take wing.
And in ashes (mournful fate!)
Death dissolves his pride and state:
Who would wish a crown to take,
Seeing that he must awake
In the dream beyond death's gate?
And the rich man dreams of gold,
Gilding cares it scarce conceals,
And the poor man dreams he feels
Want and misery and cold.
Dreams he too who rank would hold,
Dreams who bears toil's rough-ribbed hands,
Dreams who wrong for wrong demands,
And in fine, throughout the earth,
All men dream, whate'er their birth,
And yet no one understands.
'Tis a dream that I in sadness
Here am bound, the scorn of fate;
'Twas a dream that once a state
I enjoyed of light and gladness.
What is life? 'Tis but a madness.
What is life? A thing that seems,
A mirage that falsely gleams,
Phantom joy, delusive rest,
Since is life a dream at best,
And even dreams themselves are dreams.
   (*Exit*)

# ACT III

(SCENE I. *Within the Tower*)

CLARIN: In a strange enchanted tower,
I, for what I know, am prisoned;
How would ignorance be punished,
If for knowledge they would kill me?
What a thing to die of hunger,
For a man who loves good living!
I compassionate myself;
All will say: "I well believe it";
And it well may be believed,
Because silence is a virtue
Incompatible with my name
Clarin, which of course forbids it.
In this place my sole companions,
It may safely be predicted,
Are the spiders and the mice:
What a pleasant nest of linnets!—
Owing to this last night's dream,
My poor head I feel quite dizzy
From a thousand clarionets,
Shawms, and seraphines and cymbals,
Crucifixes and processions,
Flagellants who so well whipped them,
That as up and down they went,
Some even fainted as they witnessed
How the blood ran down the others.
I, if I the truth may whisper,
Simply fainted from not eating,
For I see me in this prison

## Life Is a Dream

All day wondering how this Poland
Such a *Hungary* look exhibits,
All night reading in the *Fasti*
By some half-starved poet written.
In the calendar of saints,
If a new one is admitted,
Then St. Secret be my patron,
For I fast upon his vigil;
Though it must be owned I suffer
Justly for the fault committed,
Since a servant to be silent
Is a sacrilege most sinful.
    (*A sound of drums and trumpets, with voices within*)
    (SOLDIERS *and* CLARIN)

FIRST SOLDIER: (*within*) He is here within this tower.
  Dash the door from off its hinges;
  Enter all.
CLARIN: Good God! 'tis certain
  That 'tis me they seek so briskly,
  Since they say that I am here.
  What can they require?
FIRST SOLDIER: (*within*) Go in there.
    (*Several* SOLDIERS *enter*)
SECOND SOLDIER: Here he is.
CLARIN: He's not.
ALL THE SOLDIERS: Great lord!
CLARIN: (*aside*) Are the fellows mad or tipsy?
FIRST SOLDIER: Thou art our own Prince, and we
  Will not have, and won't admit of,
  Any but our natural Prince;
  We no foreign Prince here wish for.
  Let us kneel and kiss thy feet.
THE SOLDIERS: Live, long live our best of Princes!
CLARIN: (*aside*) 'Gad! the affair grows rather serious.
  Is it usual in this kingdom
  To take some one out each day,
  Make him Prince, and then remit him
  To this tower? It must be so,

Since each day that sight I witness.
I must therefore play my part.

SOLDIERS: Thy feet give us!

CLARIN: I can't give them,
As I want them for myself.
For a prince to be a cripple
Would be rather a defect.

SECOND SOLDIER: We have all conveyed our wishes
To your father; we have told him
You alone shall be our Prince here,
Not the Duke.

CLARIN: And were you guilty
'Gainst my sire, of disrespect?

FIRST SOLDIER: 'Twas the loyalty of our spirit.

CLARIN: If 'twas loyalty, I forgive you.

SECOND SOLDIER: Come, regain thy lost dominion.
Long live Sigismund!

ALL: Live the Prince.

CLARIN: (*aside*) Say they Sigismund? Good. Admitted.
Sigismund must be the name
Given to all pretended princes.
(*Enter* SIGISMUND)

SIGISMUND: Who has named here Sigismund?

CLARIN: (*aside*) Ah, I'm but an addled prince, then!

FIRST SOLDIER: Who is Sigismund?

SIGISMUND: Who? I.

SECOND SOLDIER: (*to* CLARIN) How, then, didst thou, bold and silly,
Dare to make thee Sigismund?

CLARIN: I a Sigismund? Thou fibbest;
It was you yourselves that thus
Sigismundized me and princed me:
All the silliness and the boldness
Have been by yourselves committed.

FIRST SOLDIER: Great and brave Prince Sigismund
(For thy bearing doth convince us
Thou art he, although on faith
We proclaim thee as our prince here).

## Life Is a Dream

King Basilius, thy father,
Fearful of the Heavens fulfilling
A prediction, which declared
He would see himself submitted
At thy victor feet, attempts
To deprive thee of thy birthright,
And to give it to Astolfo,
Muscovy's duke. For this his missives
Summoned all his court: the people
Understanding, by some instinct,
That they had a natural king,
Did not wish a foreign princeling
To rule o'er them. And 'tis thus,
That the fate for thee predicted
Treating with a noble scorn,
They have sought thee where imprisoned
Thou dost live, that issuing forth,
By their powerful arms assisted,
From this tower, thy crown and scepter
Thou shouldst thus regain, and quit them
Of a stranger and a tyrant.
Forth! then; for among these cliffs here
There is now a numerous army,
Formed of soldiers and banditti,
That invoke thee: freedom waits thee;
To the thousand voices listen.

(*Voices within*) Long, long live Prince Sigismund!

SIGISMUND: Once again, O Heaven! wouldst wish me
Once again to dream of greatness
Which may vanish in an instant?
Once again to see the glories,
That a royal throne encircle,
Die in darkness and in gloom,
Like a flame the winds extinguish?
Once again by sad experience
To be taught the dangerous limits
Human power may overleap,
At its birth and while it liveth?

No, it must not, must not be:—
See me now once more submitted
To my fate: and since I know
Life is but a dream, a vision,
Hence, ye phantoms, that assume
To my darkened sense the figure
And the voice of life—although
Neither voice nor form is in them.
I no longer now desire
A feigned majesty, a fictitious
And fantastic pomp—illusions
Which the slightest breath that ripples
The calm ether can destroy,
Even as in the early spring-time,
When the flowering almond tree
Unadvisedly exhibits
All its fleeting bloom of flowers,
The first blast their freshness withers,
And the ornament and grace
Of its rosy locks disfigures.
Now I know ye—know ye all,
And I know the same false glimmer
Cheats the eyes of all who sleep.
Me false shows no more bewilder;
Disabused, I now know well
Life is but a dream—a vision.

SECOND SOLDIER: If thou thinkest we deceive thee,
Turn thine eyes to those proud cliffs here,
See the crowds that wait there, willing,
Eager to obey thee.

SIGISMUND: Yet
Just as clearly and distinctly,
I have seen another time
The same things that now I witness,
And 'twas but a dream.

SECOND SOLDIER: At all times
Great events, my lord, bring with them

## Life Is a Dream       147

Their own omens; and thy dream
But the actual fact prefigured.
SIGISMUND: You say well, it was an omen;
But supposing the bright vision
Even were true, since life is short,
Let us dream, my soul, a little,
Once again, remembering now
With all forethought and prevision
That we must once more awake
At the better time not distant;
That being known, the undeceiving,
When it comes, will be less bitter;
For it takes the sting from evil
To anticipate its visit.
And with this conviction, too,
Even its certainty admitting,
That all power being only lent
Must return unto the Giver,
Let us boldly then dare all.—
For the loyalty you exhibit,
Thanks, my lieges. See in me
One who will this land deliver
From a stranger's alien yoke.
Sound to arms; you soon shall witness
What my valor can effect.
'Gainst my father I have lifted
Hostile arms, to see if Heaven
Has of me the truth predicted.
At my feet I am to see him . . .
    (*Aside*) But if I, from dreams delivered,
Wake ere then, and nothing happens,
Silence now were more befitting.
ALL: Long live Sigismund, our king!
    (*Enter* CLOTALDO)
CLOTALDO: Ha! what tumult, heavens! has risen?
SIGISMUND: Well, Clotaldo.
CLOTALDO: Sire . . . (*Aside*) On me
  Will his wrath now fall.

CLARIN: (*aside*) He'll fling him
Headlong down the steep, I'll bet.
   (*Exit*)
CLOTALDO: At your royal feet submitted
I know how to die.
SIGISMUND: My father,
Rise, I pray, from that position,
Since to you, my guide and polestar,
Are my future acts committed;
All my past life owes you much
For your careful supervision.
Come, embrace me.
CLOTALDO: What do you say?
SIGISMUND: That I dream, and that my wishes
Are to do what's right, since we
Even in dreams should do what's fitting.
CLOTALDO: Then, my Prince, if you adopt
Acting rightly as your symbol,
You will pardon me for asking,
So to act, that you permit me.
No advice and no assistance
Can I give against my king.
Better that my lord should kill me
At his feet here.
SIGISMUND: Oh, ungrateful!
Villain! wretch! (*Aside*) But, Heavens! 'tis fitter
I restrain myself, not knowing
But all this may be a vision.—
The fidelity I envy
Must be honored and admitted.
Go and serve your lord, the king.
Where the battle rages thickest
We shall meet.—To arms, my friends!
CLOTALDO: Thanks, most generous of princes.
   (*Exit*)
SIGISMUND: Fortune, we go forth to reign;
Wake me not if this is vision,
Let me sleep not if 'tis true.

## Life Is a Dream

But which ever of them is it,
To act right is what imports me.
If 'tis true, because it is so;
If 'tis not, that when I waken
Friends may welcome and forgive me.
  (*Exeunt all, drums beating*)

  (SCENE II. *Hall in the Royal Palace*)

  (*Enter* BASILIUS *and* ASTOLFO)

BASILIUS: Who can expect, Astolfo, to restrain
An untamed steed that wildly turns to flee?
Who can the current of a stream detain,
That swollen with pride sweeps down to seek the sea?
Who can prevent from tumbling to the plain
Some mighty peak the lightning's flash sets free?
Yet each were easier in its separate way,
Than the rude mob's insensate rage to stay.
The several bands that throng each green retreat
This truth proclaim by their disparted cries;
*Astolfo* here the echoing notes repeat,
While there 'tis *Sigismund* that rends the skies.
The place where late the land was glad to greet
The choice we made, a second venture tries;
And soon will be, as Horror o'er it leans,
The fatal theater of tragic scenes.

ASTOLFO: My lord, let all this joy suspended be,
These plaudits cease, and to another day
Defer the rapture thou hast promised me;
For if this Poland (which I hope to sway)
Resists to-day my right of sovereignty,
'Tis that by merit I should win my way.
Give me a steed; to stem this wild revolt
My pride shall be the flash that bears the bolt.
  (*Exit*)

BASILIUS: Slight help there is for what is fixed by fate,
And much of danger to foresee the blow;

If it must fall, defense is then too late,
And he who most forestalls doth most foreknow.
Hard law! Stern rule! Dire fact to contemplate
That he who thinks to fly doth nearer go.
Thus by the very means that I employed,
My country and myself I have destroyed.
  (*Enter* ESTRELLA)
ESTRELLA: If, mighty lord, thy presence, which it braves,
The tumult of the crowd cannot defeat—
The frenzy of the multitude that raves
In hostile bands through every square and street,—
Thou'lt see thy kingdom swim in crimson waves,
A purple sea of blood shall round it beat;
For even already in its dismal doom
All is disaster, tragedy, and gloom.
Such is thy kingdom's ruin, so severe
The hard and bloody trial fate hath sent,
Dazed is the eye, and terrified the ear;
Dark grows the sun, and every wind is spent;
Each stone a mournful obelisk doth rear,
And every flower erects a monument;
A grave seems every house, whence life is gone,—
Each soldier is a living skeleton.
  (*Enter* CLOTALDO)
CLOTALDO: Thanks be to God, I reach thy feet alive.
BASILIUS: What news of Sigismund, Clotaldo, say?
CLOTALDO: The crowd, whom frenzy and blind impulse drive,
Into the tower resistless burst their way,
Released the Prince, who seeing thus revive
The honor he had tasted for one day,
Looked brave, declaring, in a haughty tone,
The truth at last that Heaven must now make known.
BASILIUS: Give me a horse! In person forth I'll ride
To check the pride of this ungrateful son.
Where Science erred let now the sword decide;
By my own valor shall my throne be won!
  (*Exit*)

## Life Is a Dream

ESTRELLA: Let me the glory of the fight divide—
A twinkling star beside that royal sun—
Bellona matched with Mars: for I would dare
To scale even heaven to rival Pallas there.
  (*Exit, and they sound to arms*)
  (*Enter* ROSAURA, *who detains* CLOTALDO)
ROSAURA: Though the trumpets from afar
Echo in thy valorous breast,
Hear me, list to my request,
For I know that all is war.
Well thou knowest that I came
Poor to Poland, sad, dejected;
And that graciously protected,
Thou thy pity let me claim.
It was thy command, ah, me!
I should live here thus disguised,
Striving, as thy words advised
 (Hiding all my jealousy),
To avoid Astolfo's sight;
But he saw me, and though seeing,
With Estrella, he—false being!—
Converse holds this very night
In a garden bower. The key
I have taken, and will show
Where, by entering, with a blow
Thou canst end my misery.
Thus, then, daring, bold, and strong,
Thou my honor wilt restore;
Strike, and hesitate no more,
Let his death revenge my wrong.
CLOTALDO: It is true, my inclination
Since thou first wert seen by me,
Was to strive and do for thee
 (Be thy tears my attestation)
All my life could do to serve thee.
What I first was forced to press,
Was that thou should'st change thy dress;
Lest if chancing to observe thee

Masquerading like a page,
By appearances so strong
Let astray, the Duke might wrong
By a thought thy sex and age.
Meanwhile various projects held me
In suspense, oft pondering o'er
How thy honor to restore;
Though (thy honor so compelled me)
I Astolfo's life should take—
Wild design that soon took wing—
Yet, as he was not my king,
It no terror could awake.
I his death was seeking, when
Sigismund with vengeful aim
Sought for mine; Astolfo came,
And despising what most men
Would a desperate peril deem,
Stood in my defense; his bearing,
Nigh to rashness in its daring,
Showed a valor most extreme.
How then, think, could I, whose breath
Is his gift, in murderous strife,
For his giving me my life,
Strive in turn to give him death?
And thus, grateful, yet aggrieved,
By two opposite feelings driven,
Seeing it to thee have given,
And from him have it received,
Doubting this, and that believing,
Half revenging, half forgiving,
If to thee I'm drawn by giving,
I to him am by receiving;
Thus bewildered and beset,
Vainly seeks my love a way,
Since I have a debt to pay,
Where I must exact a debt.

ROSAURA: It is settled, I believe,
As all men of spirit know,

## Life Is a Dream

That 'tis glorious to bestow,
But a meanness to receive.
Well, admitting this to be,
Then thy thanks should not be his,
Even supposing that he is
One who gave thy life to thee;
As the gift of life was thine,
And from him the taking came,
In his case the act was shame,
And a glorious act in mine.
Thus by him thou art aggrieved,
And by me even complimented,
Since to me thou hast presented
What from him thou hast received:
Then all hesitation leaving,
Thou to guard my fame shouldst fly,
Since my honor is as high
As is giving to receiving.

CLOTALDO: Though it seems a generous fever
In a noble heart to give,
Still an equal fire may live
In the heart of the receiver.
Heartlessness is something hateful,
I would boast a liberal name;
Thus I put my highest claim
In the fact of being grateful.
Then to me that title leave,—
Gentle birth breeds gentleness;
For the honor is no less
To bestow than to receive.

ROSAURA: I received my life from thee,
But for thee I now were dead;
Still it was thyself that said
No insulted life could be
Called a life: on that I stand;
Nought have I received from thee,
For the life no life could be

    That was given me by thy hand.
    But if thou wouldst first be just
    Ere being generous in this way
    (As I heard thyself once say),
    Thou wilt give me life I trust,
    Which thou hast not yet; and thus
    Giving will enhance thee more,
    For if liberal before,
    Thou wilt then be generous.
CLOTALDO: Conquered by thy argument,
    Liberal I first will be.
    I, Rosaura, will to thee
    All my property present;
    In a convent live; by me
    Has the plan been weighed some time,
    For escaping from a crime
    Thou wilt there find sanctuary;
    For so many ills present them
    Through the land on every side,
    That being nobly born, my pride
    Is to strive and not augment them.
    By the choice that I have made,
    Loyal to the land I'll be,
    I am liberal with thee,
    And Astolfo's debt is paid;
    Choose then, nay, let honor, rather,
    Choose for thee, and for us two,
    For, by Heaven! I could not do
    More for thee were I thy father!—
ROSAURA: Were that supposition true,
    I might strive and bear this blow;
    But not being my father, no.
CLOTALDO: What then dost thou mean to do?
ROSAURA: Kill the Duke.
CLOTALDO: A gentle dame,
    Who no father's name doth know,
    Can she so much valor show?

## Life Is a Dream

ROSAURA: Yes.
CLOTALDO: What drives thee on?
ROSAURA: My fame.
CLOTALDO: Think that in the Duke thou'lt see . . .
ROSAURA: Honor all my wrath doth rouse.
CLOTALDO: Soon thy king—Estrella's spouse.
ROSAURA: No, by Heaven! it must not be.
CLOTALDO: It is madness.
ROSAURA: Yes, I see it.
CLOTALDO: Conquer it.
ROSAURA: I can't o'erthrow it.
CLOTALDO: It will cost thee . . .
ROSAURA: Yes, I know it.
CLOTALDO: Life and honor.
ROSAURA: Well, so be it.
CLOTALDO: What wouldst have?
ROSAURA: My death.
CLOTALDO: Take care!
It is spite.
ROSAURA: 'Tis honor's cure.
CLOTALDO: 'Tis wild fire.
ROSAURA: That will endure.
CLOTALDO: It is frenzy.
ROSAURA: Rage, despair.
CLOTALDO: Can there then be nothing done
This blind rage to let pass by?
ROSAURA: No.
CLOTALDO: And who will help thee?
ROSAURA: I.
CLOTALDO: Is there then no remedy?
ROSAURA: None.
CLOTALDO: Think of other means whereby . . .
ROSAURA: Other means would seal my fate.
   (*Exit*)
CLOTALDO: If 'tis so, then, daughter, wait,
For together we shall die.
   (*Exit*)

(SCENE III. *The Open Plain*)

(*Enter* SIGISMUND, *clothed in skins: Soldiers marching.*
CLARIN. *Drums are heard*)

SIGISMUND: If Rome could see me on this day
  Amid the triumphs of its early sway,
  Oh, with what strange delight
  It would have seen so singular a sight,
  Its mighty armies led
  By one who was a savage wild beast bred,
  Whose courage soars so high,
  That even an easy conquest seems the sky!
  But let us lower our flight,
  My spirit; 'tis not thus we should invite
  This doubtful dream to stay,
  Lest when I wake and it has past away,
  I learn to my sad cost,
  A moment given, 'twas in a moment lost;
  Determined not to abuse it,
  The less will be my sorrow should I lose it.
  (*A trumpet sounds*)
CLARIN: Upon a rapid steed,
  (Excuse my painting it; I can't indeed
  Resist the inspiration),
  Which seems a moving mass of all creation,
  Its body being the earth,
  The fire the soul that in its heart hath birth,
  Its foam the sea, its panting breath the air,
  Chaos confused at which I stand and stare,
  Since in its soul, foam, body, breath, to me
  It is a monster made of fire, earth, air, and sea;
  Its color, dapple gray,
  Speckled its skin, and flecked, as well it may,
  By the impatient spur its flank that dyes,
  For lo! it doth not run, the meteor flies;
  As borne upon the wind,
  A beauteous woman seeks thee.

## Life Is a Dream

SIGISMUND: I'm struck blind!
CLARIN: Good God, it is Rosaura, oh, the pain!
  (*Retires*)
SIGISMUND: Heaven has restored her to my sight again.
  (*Enter* ROSAURA, *in a light corselet, with sword and dagger*)
ROSAURA: Noble-hearted Sigismund!
  Thou whose hidden light heroic
  Issues from its night of shadows
  To the great deeds of its morning;
  And as heaven's sublimest planet
  From the white arms of Aurora
  Back restores their beauteous color
  To the wild flowers and the roses,
  And upon the seas and mountains,
  When endiademed glory,
  Scatters light, diffuses splendor,
  Braids their foam, their hair makes golden;
  Thus thou dawnest on the world
  Bright auspicious sun of Poland,
  Who will help a hapless woman,
  She who at thy feet doth throw her,
  Help her, since she is unhappy,
  And a woman; two good motives
  Quite enough to move a man
  Who of valor so doth boast him,
  Though even one would be sufficient,
  Though even one would be all potent.
  Thou hast seen me thrice already,
  Thrice thou hast not truly known me,
  For each time by different dresses
  Was I strangely metamorphosed.
  First I seemed to thee a man,
  When within thy sad and somber
  Cell thou sawest me, when thy life
  Wiled from me mine own misfortunes.
  As a woman next thou sawest me,
  Where the splendors of thy throne-room

Vanished like a fleeting vision,
Vain, phantasmal and abortive.
The third time is now, when being
Something monstrous and abnormal,
In a woman's dress thou see'st me
With a warrior's arms adornéd.
And to pity and compassion
That thou may'st be moved more strongly,
Listen to the sad succession
Of my tragical misfortunes.
In the Court of Muscovy
I was born of a noble mother,
Who indeed must have been fair
Since unhappiness was her portion.
Fond and too persuading eyes
Fixed on her, a traitor lover,
Whom, not knowing, I don't name,
Though mine own worth hath informed me
What was his: for being his image,
I sometimes regret that fortune
Made me not a pagan born,
That I might, in my wild folly,
Think he must have been some god,
Such as he was, who in golden
Shower wooed Danae, or as swan
Leda loved, as bull, Europa.
When I thought to lengthen out,
Citing these perfidious stories,
My discourse, I find already
That I have succinctly told thee
How my mother, being persuaded
By the flatteries of love's homage,
Was as fair as any fair,
And unfortunate as all are.
That ridiculous excuse
Of a plighted husband's promise
So misled her, that even yet
The remembrance brings her sorrow.

# Life Is a Dream

For that traitor, that Æneas
Flying from his Troy, forgot there,
Or left after him his sword.
By this sheath its blade is covered,
But it shall be naked drawn
Ere this history is over.
From this loosely fastened knot
Which binds nothing, which ties nothing,
Call it marriage, call it crime,
Names its nature cannot alter,
I was born, a perfect image,
A true copy of my mother,
In her loveliness, ah, no!
In her miseries and misfortunes.
Therefore there is little need
To say how the hapless daughter,
Heiress of such scant good luck,
Had her own peculiar portion.
All that I will say to thee
Of myself is, that the robber
Of the trophies of my fame,
Of the sweet spoils of my honor,
Is Astolfo . . . Ah! to name him
Stirs and rouses up the choler
Of the heart, a fitting effort
When an enemy's name is spoken,—
Yes, Astolfo was that traitor,
Who, forgetful of his promise
(For when love has passed away,
Even its memory is forgotten),
Came to Poland, hither called.
From so sweet so proud a conquest,
To be married to Estrella,
Of my setting sun the torch-light.
Who'll believe that when one star
Oft unites two happy lovers,
Now one star, Estrella, comes
Two to tear from one another?

I offended, I deceived,
Sad remained, remained astonished,
Mad, half dead, remained myself;
That's to say, in so much torment,
That my heart was like a Babel
Of confusion, hell, and horror:
I resolving to be mute
(For there are some pains and sorrows
That by feelings are expressed,
Better than when words are spoken),
I by silence spoke my pain,
Till one day being with my mother
Violante, she (oh, Heavens!)
Burst their prison; like a torrent
Forth they rushed from out my breast,
Streaming wildly o'er each other.
No embarrassment it gave me
To relate them, for the knowing
That the person we confide to
A like weakness must acknowledge
Gives as 'twere to our confusion
A sweet soothing and a solace,
For at times a bad example
Has its use. In fine, my sorrows
She with pity heard, relating
Even her own grief to console me:
When he has himself been guilty
With what ease the judge condoneth!
Knowing from her own experience
That 'twas idle, to slow-moving
Leisure, to swift-fleeting time,
To intrust one's injured honor.
She could not advise me better,
As the cure of my misfortunes,
Than to follow and compel him
By prodigious acts of boldness
To repay my honor's debt:
And that such attempt might cost me

## Life Is a Dream

Less, my fortune wished that I
Should a man's strange dress put on me.
She took down an ancient sword,
Which is this I bear: the moment
Now draws nigh I must unsheath it,
Since to her I gave that promise,
When confiding in its marks,
Thus she said, "Depart to Poland,
And so manage that this steel
Shall be seen by the chief nobles
Of that land, for I have hope
That there may be one among them
Who may prove to thee a friend,
An adviser and consoler."
Well, in Poland I arrived;
It is useless to inform thee
What thou knowest already, how
A wild steed resistless bore me
To thy caverned tower, wherein
Thou with wonder didst behold me.
Let us pass, too, how Clotaldo
Passionately my cause supported,
How he asked my life of the King,
Who to him that boon accorded;
How discovering who I am
He persuaded me my proper
Dress to assume, and on Estrella
To attend as maid of honor,
So to thwart Astolfo's love
And prevent the marriage contract.
Let us, too, pass by, that here
Thou didst once again behold me
In a woman's dress, my form
Waking thus a twofold wonder,
And approach the time, Clotaldo
Being convinced it was important
That should wed and reign together
Fair Estrella and Astolfo,

'Gainst my honor, me advised
To forego my rightful project.
But, O valiant Sigismund,
Seeing that the moment cometh
For thy vengeance, since Heaven wishes
Thee to-day to burst the portals
Of thy narrow rustic cell,
Where so long immured, thy body
Was to feeling a wild beast,
Was to sufferance what the rock is,
And that 'gainst thy sire and country
Thou hast gallantly revolted,
And ta'en arms, I come to assist thee,
Intermingling the bright corselet
Of Minerva with the trappings
Of Diana, thus enrobing
Silken stuff and shining steel
In a rare but rich adornment.
On, then, on, undaunted champion!
To us both it is important
To prevent and bring to nought
This engagement and betrothal;
First to me, that he, my husband,
Should not falsely wed another,
Then to thee, that their two staffs
Being united, their jointed forces
Should with overwhelming power
Leave our doubtful victory hopeless.
Woman, I come here to urge thee
To repair my injured honor,
And as man I come to rouse thee
Crown and scepter to recover.
Woman I would wake thy pity
Since here at thy feet I throw me,
And as man, my sword and person
In thy service I devote thee.
But remember, if to-day
As a woman thou should'st court me,

## Life Is a Dream      163

I, as man, will give thee death
In the laudable upholding,
Of my honor, since I am
In this strife of love, this contest,
Woman my complaints to tell thee,
And a man to guard my honor.

SISMUND: (*aside*) Heavens! if it is true I dream,
Memory then suspend thy office,
For 'tis vain to hope remembrance
Could retain so many objects.
Help me, God! or teach me how
All these numerous doubts to conquer,
Or to cease to think of any!—
Whoe'er tried such painful problems?
If 'twas but a dream, my grandeur,
How then is it, at this moment,
That this woman can refer me
To some facts that are notorious?
Then 'twas truth, and not a dream;
But if it was truth (another
And no less confusion), how
Can my life be called in proper
Speech a dream? So like to dreams
Are then all the world's chief glories,
That the true are oft rejected
As the false, the false too often
Are mistaken for the true?
Is there then 'twixt one and the other
Such slight difference, that a question
May arise at any moment
Which is true or which is false?
Are the original and the copy
So alike, that which is which
Oft the doubtful mind must ponder?
If 'tis so, and if must vanish,
As the shades of night at morning,
All of majesty and power,
All of grandeur and of glory,

Let us learn at least to turn
To our profit the brief moment
That is given us, since our joy
Lasteth while our dream lasts only.
In my power Rosaura stands,
Thou, my heart, her charms adoreth,
Let us seize then the occasion;
Let love trample in its boldness
All the laws on which relying
She here at my feet has thrown her.
'Tis a dream; and since 'tis so,
Let us dream of joys, the sorrows
Will come soon enough hereafter.
But with mine own words just spoken,
Let me now confute myself!
If it is a dream that mocks me,
Who for human vanities
Would forego celestial glory?
What past bliss is not a dream?
Who has had his happy fortunes
Who hath said not to himself
As his memory ran o'er them,
"All I saw, beyond a doubt
Was a dream." If this exposeth
My delusion, if I know
That desire is but the glowing
Of a flame that turns to ashes
At the softest wind that bloweth;
Let us seek then the eternal,
The true fame that ne'er reposeth,
Where the bliss is not a dream,
Nor the crown a fleeting glory.
Without honor is Rosaura.
But it is a prince's province
To give honor, not to take it:
Then, by Heaven! it is her honor
That for her I must win back,
Ere this kingdom I can conquer.

## Life Is a Dream

Let us fly then this temptation.
'Tis too strong: (*To the* SOLDIERS) To arms! March onward!
For to-day I must give battle,
Ere descending night, the golden
Sunbeams of expiring day
Buries in the dark green ocean.

ROSAURA: Dost thou thus, my lord, withdraw thee?
What! without a word being spoken?
Does my pain deserve no pity?
Does my grief so little move thee?
Can it be, my lord, thou wilt not
Deign to hear, to look upon me?
Dost thou even avert thy face?

SIGISMUND: Ah, Rosaura, 'tis thy honor
That requires this harshness now,
If my pity I would show thee.
Yes, my voice does not respond,
'Tis my honor that respondeth;
True I speak not, for I wish
That my actions should speak for me;
Thee I do not look on, no,
For, alas! it is of moment,
That he must not see thy beauty
Who is pledged to see thy honor.
   (*Exit, followed by the* SOLDIERS)

ROSAURA: What enigmas, O ye skies!
After many a sigh and tear,
Thus in doubt to leave me here
With equivocal replies!

CLARIN: Madam, is it visiting hour?

ROSAURA: Welcome, Clarin, where have you been?

CLARIN: Only four stout walls between
In an old enchanted tower;
Death was on the cards for me,
But amid the sudden strife
Ere the last trump came, my life
Won the trick and I got free.
I ne'er hoped to sound again.

ROSAURA: Why?
CLARIN: Because alone I know
  Who you are: and this being so,
  Learn, Clotaldo is . . . This strain
  Puts me out.
    (*Drums are heard*)
ROSAURA: What can it be?
CLARIN: From the citadel at hand,
  Leagured round, an armed band
  As to certain victory
  Sallies forth with flags unfurled.
ROSAURA: 'Gainst Prince Sigismund! and I,
  Coward that I am, not by
  To surprise and awe the world,
  When with so much cruelty
  Each on each the two hosts spring!
    (*Exit*)
VOICES OF SOME: Live, long live our victor King!
VOICES OF OTHERS: Live, long live our liberty!
CLARIN: Live, long live the two, I say!
  Me it matters not a pin,
  Which doth lose or which doth win,
  If I can keep out of the way!—
  So aside here I will go,
  Acting like a prudent hero,
  Even as the Emperor Nero
  Took things coolly long ago.
  Or if care I cannot shun,
  Let it 'bout mine ownself be;
  Yes, here hidden I can see
  All the fighting and the fun;
  What a cozy place I spy
  Mid the rocks there! so secure,
  Death can't find me out I'm sure,
  Then a fig for death I say!
    (*Conceals himself, drums beat and the sound of arms
    heard*)
    (*Enter* BASILIUS, CLOTALDO, *and* ASTOLFO, *flying*)

## Life Is a Dream

BASILIUS: Hapless king! disastrous reign!
　Outraged father! guilty son!
CLOTALDO: See thy vanquished forces run
　In a panic o'er the plain!
ASTOLFO: And the rebel conqueror's stay,
　Proud, defiant.
BASILIUS: 'Tis decreed
　Those are loyal who succeed,
　Rebels those who lose the day.
　Let us then, Clotaldo, flee,
　Since the victory he hath won,
　From a proud and cruel son.
　　(*Shots are fired within, and* CLARIN *falls wounded from his hiding-place*)
CLARIN: Heaven protect me!
ASTOLFO: Who can be
　This last victim of the fight,
　Who struck down in the retreat,
　Falls here bleeding at our feet?
CLARIN: I am an unlucky wight,
　Who to shun Death's fearful face
　Found the thing I would forget:
　Flying from him, him I've met.
　For there is no secret place
　Hid from death; and therefore I
　This conclusion hold as clear,
　He 'scapes best who goes more near,
　He dies first who first doth fly.
　Then return, return and be
　In the bloody conflict lost;
　Where the battle rages most,
　There is more security
　Than in hills how desolate,
　Since no safety can there be
　'Gainst the force of destiny,
　And the inclemency of fate;
　Therefore 'tis in vain thou flyest
　From the death thou draw'st more nigh,

Oh, take heed for thou must die
If it is God's will thou diest!
   (*Falls within*)
BASILIUS: Oh, take heed for thou must die
If it is God's will thou diest!—
With what eloquence, O Heaven!
Does this body that here lieth,
Through the red mouth of a wound
To profoundest thoughts entice us
From our ignorance and our error!
The red current as it glideth
Is a bloody tongue that teaches
All man's diligence is idle,
When against a greater power,
And a higher cause it striveth.
Thus with me, 'gainst strife and murder
When I thought I had provided,
I but brought upon my country
All the ills I would have hindered.
CLOTALDO: Though, my lord, fate knoweth well
Every path, and quickly findeth
Whom it seeks; yet still it strikes me
'Tis not Christian-like to say
'Gainst its rage that nought suffices.
That is wrong, a prudent man
Even o'er fate victorious rises;
And if thou art not preserved
From the ills that have surprised thee,
From worse ills thyself preserve.
ASTOLFO: Sire, Clotaldo doth address thee
As a cautious, prudent man,
Whose experience time hath ripened.
I as a bold youth would speak:
Yonder, having lost its rider,
I behold a noble steed
Wandering reinless and unbridled,
Mount and fly with him while I
Guard the open path behind thee.

## Life Is a Dream

BASILIUS: If it is God's will I die,
Or if Death for me here lieth
As in ambush, face to face
I will meet it and defy it.
  (*Enter* SIGISMUND, ESTRELLA, ROSAURA, SOLDIERS *and* ATTENDANTS)
A SOLDIER: 'Mid the thickets of the mountain,
'Neath these dark boughs so united,
The King hides.
SIGISMUND: Pursue him then,
Leave no single shrub unrifled,
Nothing must escape your search,
Not a plant, and not a pine tree.
CLOTALDO: Fly, my lord!
BASILIUS: And wherefore fly?
ASTOLFO: Come!
BASILIUS: Astolfo, I'm decided.
CLOTALDO: What to do?
BASILIUS: To try, Clotaldo,
One sole remedy that surviveth.
  (*To* SIGISMUND) If 'tis me thou'rt seeking, Prince,
At thy feet behold me lying.
  (*Kneeling*)
Let thy carpet be these hairs
Which the snows of age have whitened.
Tread upon my neck, and trample
On my crown; in base defilement
Treat me with all disrespect;
Let thy deadliest vengeance strike me
Through my honor; as thy slave
Make me serve thee, and in spite of
All precautions let fate be,
Let Heaven keep the word it plighted.
SIGISMUND: Princes of the Court of Poland,
Who such numerous surprises
Have astonished seen, attend,
For it is your prince invites ye.
That which heaven has once determined,

That which God's eternal finger
Has upon the azure tablets
Of the sky sublimely written,
Those transparent sheets of sapphire
Superscribed with golden ciphers
Ne'er deceive, and never lie;
The deceiver and the liar
Is he who to use them badly
In a wrongful sense defines them.
Thus, my father, who is present,
To protect him from the wildness
Of my nature, made of me
A fierce brute, a human wild beast;
So that I, who from my birth,
From the noble blood that trickles
Through my veins, my generous nature,
And my liberal condition,
Might have proved a docile child,
And so grew, it was sufficient
By so strange an education,
By so wild a course of living,
To have made my manners wild;—
What a method to refine them!
If to any man 'twas said,
"It is fated that some wild beast
Will destroy you," would it be
Wise to wake a sleeping tiger
As the remedy of the ill?
If 'twere said, "This sword here hidden
In its sheath, which thou dost wear,
Is the one foredoomed to kill thee,"
Vain precaution it would be
To preserve the threatened victim.
Bare to point it at his breast.
If 'twere said, "These waves that ripple
Calmly here for thee will build
Foam-white sepulchers of silver,"
Wrong it were to trust the sea

## Life Is a Dream

When its haughty breast is lifted
Into mountain heights of snow,
Into hills of curling crystal.
Well, this very thing has happened
Unto him, who feared a wild beast,
And awoke him while he slept;
Or who drew a sharp sword hidden
Naked forth, or dared the sea
When 'twas roused by raging whirlwinds
And though my fierce nature (hear me)
Was as 'twere the sleeping tiger,
A sheathed sword my innate rage,
And my wrath a quiet ripple,
Fate should not be forced by means
So unjust and so vindictive,
For they but excite it more;
And thus he who would be victor
O'er his fortune, must succeed
By wise prudence and self-strictness.
Not before an evil cometh
Can it rightly be resisted
Even by him who hath foreseen it,
For although (the fact's admitted)
By an humble resignation
It is possible to diminish
Its effects, it first must happen,
And by no means can be hindered.
Let it serve as an example
This strange sight, this most surprising
Spectacle, this fear, this horror,
This great prodigy; for none higher
E'er was worked than this we see,
After years of vain contriving,
Prostrate at my feet a father,
And a mighty king submitted.
This the sentence of high Heaven
Which he did his best to hinder
He could not prevent. Can I,

Who in valor and in science,
Who in years am so inferior,
It avert? (*To the King*) My lord, forgive me,
Rise, sir, let me clasp thy hand;
For since Heaven has now apprized thee
That thy mode of counteracting
Its decree was wrong, a willing
Sacrifice to thy revenge
Let my prostrate neck be given.

BASILIUS: Son, this noble act of thine
In my heart of hearts reviveth
All my love, thou'rt there reborn.
Thou art Prince; the bay that bindeth
Heroes' brows, the palm, be thine,
Let the crown thine own deeds give thee.

ALL: Long live Sigismund our King!

SIGISMUND: Though my sword must wait a little
Ere great victories it can gain,
I to-day will win the highest,
The most glorious, o'er myself.—
Give, Astolfo, give your plighted
Hand here to Rosaura, since
It is due and I require it.

ASTOLFO: Though 'tis true I owe the debt,
Still 'tis needful to consider
That she knows not who she is;
It were infamous, a stigma
On my name to wed a woman . . .

CLOTALDO: Stay, Astolfo, do not finish;
For Rosaura is as noble
As yourself. My sword will right her
In the field against the world:
She's my daughter, that's sufficient.

ASTOLFO: What do you say?

CLOTALDO: Until I saw her
To a noble spouse united,
I her birth would not reveal.

## Life Is a Dream

It were now a long recital,
But the sum is, she's my child.
ASTOLFO: That being so, the word I've plighted
I will keep.
SIGISMUND: And that Estrella
May not now be left afflicted,
Seeing she has lost a prince
Of such valor and distinction,
I propose from mine own hand
As a husband one to give her,
Who, if he does not exceed
Him in worth, perhaps may rival
Give to me thy hand.
ESTRELLA: I gain
By an honor so distinguished.
SIGISMUND: To Clotaldo, who so truly
Served my father, I can give him
But these open arms wherein
He will find whate'er he wishes.
A SOLDIER: If thou honorest those who serve thee,
Thus, to me the first beginner
Of the tumult through the land,
Who from out the tower, thy prison,
Drew thee forth, what wilt thou give?
SIGISMUND: Just that tower: and that you issue
Never from it until death,
I will have you guarded strictly;
For the traitor is not needed
Once the treason is committed.
BASILIUS: So much wisdom makes one wonder.
ASTOLFO: What a change in his condition!
ROSAURA: How discreet! how calm! how prudent!
SIGISMUND: Why this wonder, these surprises,
If my teacher was a dream,
And amid my new aspirings
I am fearful I may wake,
And once more a prisoner find me
In my cell? But should I not,

Even to dream it is sufficient:
For I thus have come to know
That at last all human blisses
Pass and vanish as a dream,
And the time that may be given me
I henceforth would turn to gain:
Asking for our faults forgiveness,
Since to generous, noble hearts
It is natural to forgive them.

# NONE BENEATH
# THE KING

# Rojas Zorrilla

Francisco de Rojas Zorrilla was born in Toledo in 1607 and died in Madrid forty-one years later. Little is known with certainty about his life except that following an old Spanish—perhaps a universal—custom, he is reported to have had many love affairs in and out of wedlock. As a writer he was popular in both Spain and France. Shortly before his death he was made a knight of the Order of Santiago.

As a dramatist Rojas Zorrilla was influenced by both Lope and Calderón, but he belonged decidedly to the Calderonian school. In fact, he even collaborated with him on some plays. Though not on a par with Lope or Calderón, Zorrilla was one of the most sublime Spanish dramatists of the *Siglo de Oro*. He was influenced by Lope in his varied, complicated and amazing fertility of plot construction, and by Calderón in the treatment of the *pundonor* and the use of affected, artificial language and sweet and delicate lyricism. Zorrilla excelled both Lope and Calderón in the perceptive delineation of women, in the delightful use of the comic element and in the skillful handling of the *capa y espada* (cloak and dagger) genre. Unlike his idol, Calderón, however, Zorrilla was careless and uneven. Zorrilla was a favorite of both the ruling class and of the common people; the former, because he made ample and flattering use of courtiers and palaces in his plays, and the latter, because of the ingenious originality and daring situations of his plots and of his respect for the popular rights.

Unlike Lope and Calderón, especially the former, Zorrilla was not prolific in his literary production. The maximum number of works attributed to him does not exceed sixty, embracing all types—tragedies, comedies, farces (*entremeses*) and allegorical or religious plays (*autos sacramentales*). However, he was rather versatile, equally effective in the various genres —in sweet simplicity of expression as well as in rhetorical inflation—and in light and heavy treatment of themes and characters. The outstanding quality of his writings is his originality and his inventiveness, carried even to daring extremes. He did not imitate any of his contemporaries, although many of his contemporaries, including some famous French dramatists, often plagiarized his plots.

*Del Rey Abajo Ninguno* (*None Beneath the King*) perpetuates the deserved fame of its author.

# None Beneath the King
(*Del Rey Abajo Ninguno*)

This play had three different titles: (1) *Del Rey Abajo Ninguno* (*None Beneath the King*), (2) *García del Castañar* (the name of the hero, a peasant at Castañar near Toledo), and (3) *El Labrador Más Honrado* (*The Most Honorable Peasant*), but it is best known by the first title. It is regarded as Rojas Zorrilla's masterpiece and his most popular drama. It is a model of the *comedia de capa y espada* (cloak and dagger play) and one of the most effective of the Spanish comedias dealing with the *pundonor* (point of honor). It has been characterized as "the most modern drama in its structure that can be found in the old Spanish theatre."

Its chief motif is the conflict between Spanish honor and Spanish loyalty. According to the thinking of the Spaniards of that day, in consonance with the prevailing theory of the divine origin of royalty, a king could do no wrong; therefore only the King (but no one else) was justified in tarnishing conjugal honor. The plot turns on mistaken identity and unfolds as follows: García, a wealthy, generous and loyal peasant lives in a state of quiet retirement in the town of Castañar with his faithful and beloved wife, Blanca. One day the neighborhood is visited by the King, who is traveling incognito accompanied by several courtiers. One of the latter, named Mendo, happens to be wearing the royal red sash, a circumstance which leads García to mistake him for the real king, whom he does not know. Mendo falls in love with Blanca. One night, thinking that García was away, the courtier gains entrance into the lady's apartment. García unexpectedly appears, but believing the intruder and would-be seducer to be the King, refrains from avenging the dishonor. Since the King may not be slain, for he is God's representative on earth and answerable only to the Lord, the wife must die, in accordance with the prevailing code of honor. She manages to escape to the royal palace, pursued by her husband. When García enters the palace and sees the real King as well as the offending courtier, he slays the latter, for beneath the King no one is exempt from the vengeance which must be wreaked by the man whose honor has been tarnished.

The story, however, is not what makes this play memorable. Its chief merits derive from the masterful character sketches, excellent descriptions, graceful versification, smoothly flowing dialogue, and natural, well-balanced development of the action. It owes its lasting popularity to the indisputable fact that it is one of the most poetical and most profoundly national plays in the Spanish language.

# NONE BENEATH THE KING

# Characters

| | |
|---|---|
| GARCÍA | *farmer* |
| BLANCA | *farmer's wife* |
| TERESA | *farmer* |
| BELARDO | *old man* |
| THE KING | *Alfonso XI of Castile* |
| THE QUEEN | *María of Portugal* |
| MENDO | *courtier* |
| BRAS | *rustic* |
| COUNT OF ORGAZ | *old man* |
| TELLO | *servant* |
| TWO COURTIERS | |
| MUSICIANS AND FARMERS | |

*Period: 14th Century*

# ACT I

(SCENE I. *At the Court*)

(*Enter the* KING, *a red sash across his breast, reading a petition.* DON MENDO *follows*)

KING: Don Mendo, I have witnessed your request.
MENDO: Say rather my complaint, wherein I beg that I receive the knighthood of the sash: the selfsame grace I craved two months agone. Ten years within the palace walls I've served, another ten upon the battlefield; such is the 'prenticeship you have ordained for him who would attain the coveted insignia that you so nobly bear. I find, Milord, upon my own account, that I am thereto eligible. Else, my asking were but begging thanks for insult. You promised to investigate my claim, and I deserve your favor, worthy sire,—without it is my noble blood besmirched.
KING: Don Mendo, call the count.
MENDO: And to my prayer?
KING: 'Tis well. The count . . .
MENDO: He comes.
KING: Pray draw aside. (*Enter the* COUNT *with a paper*)
MENDO: 'Tis well that I have asked him for the sash, nor should I so have done, if, first of all I had not made my own investigation.
KING: (*to Count*) What news?
COUNT: In Algeciras all is fear before your sword, while fell Grenada's chief rouses all Africa to treacherous plots.
KING: And what financial aid comes to the realm?

COUNT: Engrossed upon this parchment may you read, Milord, the faithful kingdom's bounteous gifts.

KING: And the investigation which I bade you make in secret, worthy Count, of one Don Mendo. Is it made?

COUNT: It is, Milord.

KING: Indeed. With what success? Tell me the truth.

COUNT: I find that he is full as good as I.

KING: And those with whom he served the kingdom's cause— are they sufficient to this enterprise?

COUNT: A mighty check, Alphonso, will you be unto the black moor's arrogance.

KING: I wish to learn, Orgaz, the names of those who own my gratitude for their prompt aid. Read, then.

COUNT: May you in peace be crowned where sweet Genil washes its golden sands.

KING: Heaven guard thee well, our Christian Mars. Don Mendo, prithee read.

MENDO: Thus runs it: "What the loyal land subscribes unto the Algeciras enterprise, given in horses, silver, and in men. Don Gil of Albornoz, ten thousand soldiers, all quartered at his personal expense; Orgaz, two thousand; Count Astorga, too, will head four thousand; sixteen thousand more the cities grant, full paid; and with their men the three Castilian brotherhoods will march to the Genil. Count Aguilar donates a thousand prancing steeds, all fleet of foot, and adds a thousand ducats unto that; García of Castañar begs leave to send a hundred hundredweight of salted meat, two thousand bushels of flour, four thousand more of barley, likewise forty casks of wine, three flocks of cattle, a hundred infantry, and even a hundred hundredweight of bacon. 'This little' (he says) 'I send because the year has been a scanty one. But such I give, and, if I worthy be, offer my king a rustic heart, a law-abiding soul, who, though the king he knows not, knows full well the loyal vassal's aid which is his due.'"

KING: How rich in presents and in loyalty!

MENDO: A humble title, this,—of Castañar.

KING: And tell me, Count, where does this subject live?

COUNT: I pray your Highness, listen who this is: five leagues

# None Beneath the King

from famed Toledo, country mine and your great court, there lies a verdant vale called Castañar, where dwells this countryman, surrounded by a lofty mountain chain whose tops bow ancient fealty to Spain. Adown this lowland, nestled at the foot of overtowering hills, a convent stands, named for Assisi's knight, Christ's other self. For, such humility St. Francis dons, that, even at the bottom of a hill he rears his dwelling. In the meadow's bounds a chestnut patch extends, whence comes the name of Castañar to convent, vale and man. Here, like to Abraham, sweet charity he sows, while heaven and he in rivalry contend to see whose harvest most will yield. Close by the convent is his country seat, three parts in all,—the first, his rustic home, well stocked with wine and olives,—gold with corn. Indeed, so great his heaven-sent gift of wheat, the granaries of Spain are but as anthills, compared unto the bounty of his lofts. Second, a garden, whose fair blooming flowers are fragrant daughters of the sun and earth; so varied they in color and so bright, that from their radiance it would appear the fourth sphere sent its stars in them to shine. Thirdly, a room, formed like a gallery, buttressed on arches three of St. Paul's jaspar; above are balconies in green and gold, the slated roof capped by pure emerald globes. Here dwells García with his happy spouse, Blanca by name, in whose fair arms he shares the sweetest life which ever Love bestowed, his boons contending with his happiness. Her beauty, envied of the sun, I leave for those of younger heart and rosier days. Let it suffice to say that all his wealth is poverty itself compared to her. A lusty kinsman he, a hunter bold who holds his own in combat with a bull. Nor has he yet beheld your royal gaze, but flees your sight, affirming that the king is as the sun, which blinds with too much light. Such is García of Castañar; in faith, if you retain him in the coming war, you hold beside you prudence as a guide, the truth immaculate, with foresight keen, a wealthy man without ambition's goad, too, unobtrusive,—wit with daring, a staunch and upright countryman, withal.

KING: Remarkable, indeed!

COUNT: Upon my word I'll wager that the qualities I've named would go, at court, to make a perfect knight.
KING: And you say he has never seen me?
COUNT: Never.
KING: Then must I see him,—learn perforce to know him—I and Don Mendo with two others,—for the road is short and we shall take along the swooping falcons so that we may feign we go a-hunting. On this very day I fare to Castañar and speak with him in such a way that he shall not suspect my royalty. What say you, Count, to this?
COUNT: Your wit is matched to the occasion's need.
KING: Prepare the horses, Count.
COUNT: Milord, your servant.
   (*Exit. Enter the* QUEEN)
MENDO: Her Highness enters.
QUEEN: Whither now, Milord?
KING: To seek a hidden treasure which the count has brought to light.
QUEEN: And is it far?
KING: In Castañar.
QUEEN: And when shall you return?
KING: As soon as is the metal well assayed within the crucible.
QUEEN: I grieve your absence.
KING: Before the sun shines o'er the mountain heights I shall return, Milady, to my sphere.
QUEEN: Absence is night.
KING: And you are as the day.
QUEEN: You are my sun.
KING: And my aurora, you.
MENDO: And what reply to my request?
KING: Don Mendo, content with your nobility's proud worth, today I place this sash upon your breast. In honor do I grant it, and perchance, should it adorn an undeserving heart it would become a stain and lose its hue—an insult to the nobles, since I bore to have the lowly wear it. Should I grant its honored red amain, its worth would sink to nothing, shared by all, esteemed by none.

## None Beneath the King

(SCENE II. *At Castañar*)

GARCÍA: Homestead mine, fair blessed country dwelling, where bides a happy, yet unhappy soul. Since that day when the conquering Spanish host with timely faith crowned child Alphonso king within his cradle,—since then am I hidden. Resting in thee, content to leave behind the splendors of the court, to till the fields, wherein I hide my noble birth. I came a wandering exile, and as friend remained. Within thy sacred walls, midst plenteous wealth, I live content with my adoréd spouse, whose mantle decks a noble pedigree, although its source is still to me unknown. Yet do I know her virtue, and adore her beauty, nurtured in the friendly home of wise Orgaz the farmer. There I saw her, and one fair day she smote me, even as does the lightning. I was ashes all within, yet sound to outward view. In my distress I sought the count, and he assured me prompt that in her veins there coursed a noble blood. I wedded her, and found my honor there, having at first consulted, as is just, propriety, before requiting passion. With her I live a happy life, what though I know not who she is, nor yet does she know my nobility. My loving Blanca, disporting now amidst her simple folk, and weaving, from her garden, chaplets fair of jessamine, to gird her forehead's crown! The quivering air announces her approach, by joyous laughter heralded, and music. (*Enter* BLANCA, *with flowers, followed by* BRAS, TERESA, BELARDO, *musicians and shepherds*)

### MUSIC

*Fair is she as is the sun,*
*Brighter than the snow.*
*Beautiful her radiance*
*Even as the sun.*
*In the morning she arises,*
*Even as the sun,*
*Flooding all the fields with light,*
*Even as the sun.*
*Beside her cheek the snow is dark,*

*And black the blossom of the almond;
She is fair as is the sun,
Brighter than the snow.*

GARCÍA: My Blanca, cherished mate,—what cruelty—if, to give life unto these budding flowers, you take *my* life,—yourself,—away from me!

BLANCA: How can I, treading on them, give them life? Adored mate, when I am not with you my life is absent. So much do I love, that knowing your deep passion unto me, if you should lose your life, you well could live with my life, which forever must be yours.

GARCÍA: What grace, however great, what favoring deed, pretends to aught when measured by my love!

BLANCA: So much you love me, then?

GARCÍA: Yes, Blanca, hear me.
The mower loves not more the cooling breeze,
My sowings love not more the April shower,
My cattle love not more the valley's herb,
Nor love my shepherds more the sheltering leaf;
Nor loves the sufferer more the light of day,
The laboring cowherds more the shades of night,
The rolling meadows more the runnel's crystal,
Than I love you, beloved Blanca mine.
If all earth's loves, since Adam first appeared,
Unto this day, should merge their fires in one,
Still should my passion burn with brighter flame.
And though I find my all-absorbing faith
Full answered in your heart, I can not love
More than I do, though your deserts be more.

BLANCA: The flowers love not more the morning dew,
When sips the sun within their fragrant chalice;
The treetops love not more the feathery snowflakes
Which fall as crystal, melting then to rivers.
The frozen North compels not more the magnet,
The rainbow's arc the traveler in the rain,
Nor counsels lurking night the traitorous deed,
More than I love you, sweet defender mine.

# None Beneath the King

So great my love is, to your very name,
As to a thing divine I'd raise a shrine
Where I might worship it. Affright you not,
Did I not know that God dwells high above,
No longer would I love you as a man,
But I should hold you, worship you, as God.

BRAS: Since Blanca and García coo like doves, let us, too, bill and coo, for by my soul, since I gazed on you the other day your pretty little face has turned my head.

TERESA: Your figure pleases me, I must confess.

BRAS: I swear, I love you more than you do me.

TERESA: Indeed! Not so!

BRAS: Then listen, dear Teresa. One day I saw you as I passed the brook, and helped you wring the dripping table-cloths; so well we washed, and excellently wrung, a student on the way told us, "Just so a lawyer leaves his client." You're as dear to me as is unto a usurer the life of one who by his life has sworn.

(*Exeunt* BELARDO, *musicians and shepherds. Enter* TELLO)

TELLO: García, the happiest should envy you, in whom alone there reigns such calm repose.

BLANCA: What news, Tello?

TELLO: Fair lady mine, from whom exhales the fragrance of the jessamine, the count begs leave to kiss your worthy hand.

BLANCA: How fares the count?

TELLO: As ever at your service.

GARCÍA: Inform us, Tello, what cause leads him here?

TELLO: I'll answer privately. Today the count commissioned me to bring with all due haste this letter to you. There is no reply. 'Tis all. I must be off.

GARCÍA: You'll not remain?

TELLO: I'd gladly stop with you another day, but those who fast approach must see me not. Good bye.

GARCÍA: (*aside*) The missive is addressed to me. Perhaps in anger at the scanty aid I sent the king. But, here is how it reads: "Señor García, the king has seen your gift, and asked, in admiration, who you are. I answered that you were a countryman, reserved, discreet. Now comes he secretly to test your prudence and your bravery. You must not show him that you understand, nor yet must he discover who you are; for though I do command his ministry, yet has your father wronged him, and I know what anger his mere memory invokes. Farewell. And this remember—that the king is he who wears the sash of red. Your friend, Count of Orgaz." Ah! Did the king but know whose son I am, how could I turn from me the punishment which my dead father earned?

BLANCA: My love, such silence, such deep perturbation betoken sorrow's tidings. Tell me all.

GARCÍA: This letter, Blanca, sent me by the count, but bids me welcome to our home some guests.

BLANCA: And well you may. Our house is ever open.

BRAS: From off three thunderbolts adorned with manes, comets of Spanish breed with dangling tails, or birds of flight,—in fact, fleet-footed steeds, who trot right well yet who can fly but ill, four stately gentlemen, in hunter's garb, have just alighted in the court without.

GARCÍA: Let them not know that you have told us so.

TERESA: Just see! What handsome figures each one has!

BRAS: Egad! I tell you,—gallant company!

(*Enter the* KING, *without the sash, and* DON MENDO, *with a sash, followed by* TWO HUNTSMEN)

GARCÍA: (*aside*) I see who of them wears the given sign. (*Aloud*) Fair sirs of noble race, may Heaven grant its fairest gifts and honors unto you. Command me.

MENDO: Tell us, prithee, who is he García of Castañar by name?

GARCÍA: 'Tis I. And at your service.

MENDO: Faith, a hardy wight.

GARCÍA: The good Lord made me so.

BRAS: Nor overlook the fact that I head all his swineherds. And have no small worth, so that if I can serve the gentlemen within my sphere of duty, with ill grace will I do it, as the deed will forthwith specify.

GARCÍA: Away, you beast!

## None Beneath the King

BRAS: I, beast! This is too much!
KING: What simple ways. Heaven guard you well.
GARCÍA: Though I know not your name, your person lends you favor in my eyes.
BRAS: A very jewel he,—I like him, too.
MENDO: We chased a flying raven through the wood, and all fatigued we spied your welcome roof at Castañar. So thither are we come to view it, and to rest us here a while, until the sun sinks 'neath the western sky.
GARCÍA: You'll find the house quite large for such as we, yet must it be too mean for such as you. However, its defects will be redeemed by service gladly given,—sincerely felt.
MENDO: And do you know us?
GARCÍA: No, in very truth,—for we have never wandered from this place.
MENDO: We four are chamber valets to the king, and at your bidding. Who is this fair lady?
GARCÍA: My wife.
MENDO: Dear lady, for a thousand years may you enjoy such company as his. And may kind Heaven send you an offspring more than all the seeds you sow across the fields.
BLANCA: Not few, indeed, upon my word.
MENDO: Your name?
BLANCA: 'Tis Blanca.*
MENDO: Well it matches with your beauty.
BLANCA: Exposure to the air is beauty's bane.
KING: I too, fair Blanca, add my humble wish that both may live for endless centuries, and from your children may you see succeed grandchildren numbering more than all the trees upon this range,—that your posterity will scarce find room to dwell within these lands.
BRAS: Sooth! Let them cease this prattle. Much they heed their idle speech! With peopling thus the fields, where shall my roving swine find space to breathe?
GARCÍA: My folk will entertain with rustic sport, as the occasion offers. So I pray accept my modest hospitality. Prepare, then, Blanca mine, a good repast.

---
*i.e. White, or fair.

MENDO: *(aside)* García, call her Fire; she's burned my hear[t]
KING: 'Tis honor to accept such courtesy.
GARCÍA: I'd serve the king himself with equal will. Though [I]
have never seen him, yet would I most gladly pay hi[s]
tribute.
KING: Tell me, then, have you good grounds for shunning [?]
his sight?
GARCÍA: Ah, that were long to tell—another time. You,—
Blanca, Bras, Teresa,—prithee go and set our trifling fa[re]
upon the board.

*(Exeunt* BLANCA, BRAS, *and* TERESA*)*

KING: I am informed the king has heard of you.
MENDO: Aye—both of us stand witness unto that.
GARCÍA: The king—to bother with a lowly peasant?
KING: And so much he esteems the proffered aid sent lately [to]
the crown,—namely, yourself to go to Algeciras in the wa[r]
—that were you but to follow him to court, he'd grant yo[u]
at his side the highest post,—the place most envied in th[e]
royal suite.
GARCÍA: What say you? I would rather rise at dawn an[d]
girded with my trusty arquebuse, make chase across th[e]
undulating hills after a flock of frightened partridges; m[y]
eager hounds rush on in hot pursuit, while all my sense[s]
pulse hard at the game, following valley up and valle[y]
down to see the wounded flyers fall to ground. And whe[n]
I see the hazy clouds of grey beating their wings and shov[v]-
ing feet of red, I seize a scattered few and watch in gle[e]
my panting dogs run off to fetch the rest (excited at th[e]
voice of my command), and bring the game, still war[m]
with life, to me. I take it from their mouths, and seek to fin[d]
just where the lead has pierced the feathered wing. The[n]
turn I home, proud as the conquering count when he come[s]
back, a victor, to Toledo. Now is the feast.—The birds ar[e]
straightway plucked, broiled o'er the coals and put upo[n]
the spit, adorned with six small slices of choice ham. Thre[e]
turns or four, and lo—a firey bit as red as ever cinnamo[n]
from Brazil. Then Teresa, seasoning the birds with spice[,]
pepper, vinegar and oil, and dresses them upon my humbl[e]

board, where, offering up our thanks unto the Lord, we eat our fare, my loving wife and I, each taking one,—for nothing can compare with sharing two cooked partridges 'twixt two. Betimes Teresa gets a morsel, too, less for herself than to make envious Bras; and then I fling the hounds a juicy bone, and hear the music of their crunching teeth intent upon their relish. Then I toast my tender Blanca in a sparkling glass of crystal water—even so she replies,—and leaving thus the table, render grace to Him who sends to us our daily bread. Such, then, is Castañar, which I do love far more than all that kings could ever give.

KING: How comes it, then, that loving so your home, you offer yet your person for the war?

GARCÍA: Your pardon, sir, you do not understand. The king, in times of harsh necessity, owns every man-of-honor's life and wealth. And now, with burning zeal, he turns his way to Algeciras, scant in arms and funds, to extirpate the foreign infidel. And that is why I offered up my life,—not for ambition in duty bound. Because he needs me, thus, as is his due, I gave my life to whose life it is, nor do I wait until he first must call.

KING: And when the war is past, you'll not remain at court?

GARCÍA: Our life is here open and this fare blessed by constant people.

KING: It may well be the king shall give you a sovereign post.

GARCÍA: And would that make it just for peasants to receive another's right.

KING: The king may choose his favorites whence he will.

GARCÍA: Perhaps 'tis so—it cannot be with us. A perilous friendship his, and well I know that he is least secure whom most he loves; and I have always heard it said of court that king's friends run more risk than enemies,—for one confides, another keeps his trouble. I had a father, loyal to the king, who gave me counsel oft, and he affirmed with certainty, the king was like a flame which warmed from far, but which from near did burn.

KING: And yet, 'tis said by many that the king, even as God, can mould from lowly clay a nobleman of universal worth.

GARCÍA: Of clay have many made, and broken too.
KING: That work must well have been an imperfection.
GARCÍA: Then have it as you will,—what can the king gi[ve]
  unto one who has no earthly wish?
KING: Can he not favor him?
GARCÍA: And punish him, too.
KING: He can grant authority . . .
GARCÍA: And furnish cares.
KING: He can shower wealth . . .
GARCÍA: And those to envy it.
KING: Show graces.
GARCÍA: And keen enemies to boot. Nor need you tire yourse[lf]
  with your account. I know my needs, and would not chan[ge]
  my lot, even could I purchase all the royal boons with o[ne]
  green blade of grass from Castañar. All this without th[e]
  slightest rancor said against his regal splendors. But I vo[w]
  I quite forgot the matter of our meal.
  (*Exit* GARCÍA)
KING: The count did not exaggerate. This man exceeds th[e]
  high opinion I had formed.
MENDO: A charming house.
KING: Extremely. Can you tell what is there here which mo[st]
  compels your eyes?
MENDO: If I must own the truth, I do confess it is the beau[ty]
  of García's wife.
KING: How radiant she is!
MENDO: How heavenly! A gleaming angel, of snow-whi[te]
  purity.
KING: Can this be love?
MENDO: Who ever scoffed at beauty?
KING: Cover your head, Don Mendo, and recall that here m[y]
  majesty must be concealed.
MENDO: You veil the splendor of your royal rays, receivin[g]
  homage for your private worth. So much, that from you[r]
  breast you have removed the sash of red, the better to con[-]
  ceal yourself, and lend new grandeur unto me.
KING: Cover your head. They must not know us here. W[e]
  must dissemble.

## None Beneath the King

MENDO: Rich man I indeed, and henceforth proud grandee before your eyes*
KING: Since I have spoken, I will not retract.

(*Enter* DOÑA BLANCA)

BLANCA: I pray you, enter, sirs, to dine with us. The table, decked with flowers of spring, awaits.
MENDO: And what shall we receive?
BLANCA: Why should you ask? Eat what there is, for payment there is none, or else go hungry. In a peasant's home there never lacks good cheese, fine must and olives, and furthermore I promise you white bread,—I and Teresa kneaded it, you know. Why! Such a fare would appetize the dead! The early fruitage of a tender vine, sweet dewy honey and Toledan pears, and tasty partridges preserved in brine. Moreover, though the sight be none too fair, a boar's head neatly trimmed in jellied fruit,—for every product has its own good use; good sausages that follow well with wine, two ducks and freshly salted meat a-plenty, whose fibres quite resemble leafless pinks, that, one by one, like silk of crimson hue might well be woven on the spinning wheel.
KING: Then let us enter, Blanca.
BLANCA: Follow me, and may good appetite wait on your meal.

(*Exeunt the* KING *and the* TWO HUNTSMEN)

MENDO: Fair country dame, who ever gazed on you and did not love?
BLANCA: Pray enter and keep silence.
MENDO: How gladly would I give all you describe for one small dish well seasoned with your love.
BLANCA: Then tell me, wearer of the sash of red, what plate I may prepare for you.
MENDO: Your hand.
BLANCA: A cow's foot dressed in sauce were daintier far. May Heaven preserve my hand—amen to that. Nor should you wish for such a lowly fare. A peasant's hand is too mean for a lord.

---
*i.e. Because none but a grandee has the right to stand covered in the presence of the king.

MENDO: Your will would season it unto my lips.

BLANCA: Your pardon, sir, St. Peter is at Rome. And if yo‹
know it not, I tell you now that such a dish is for n‹
spouse alone, who well repays it, nor who needs to stoo‹
to flattery and ill-directed speech.

MENDO: I, too, can pay with station and luxury.

BLANCA: Expend your vanities on better ventures. The gypsi‹
would not buy García's wife, for she is coarse and rusti‹

MENDO: And as fair as sweetest blossom.

BLANCA: If you wish to know from whence I spring, it is fro‹
old Orgaz, and at your service.

MENDO: Heaven gave you your beauty, the mountains adde‹
such relentlessness.

BLANCA: The ladies of our land are far from fools. To tabl‹
then, and may you eat your fill.

MENDO: You will not understand me, Blanca mine?

BLANCA: I understand full well your song's refrain. Orga‹
woman is not quite so dull.

MENDO: Then by your lovely eyes, you'll hear my plea!

BLANCA: Do not disturb the feast. Enter within, for all a‹
seated. Be more courteous.

MENDO: And you less obdurate.

BLANCA: You'll not desist? Then listen: Here, García, con‹
you here!

(*Enter* GARCÍA)

GARCÍA: What would you have, my eyes' delight?

BLANCA: I pray, do send this guest within. He will not cea‹
to spin the endless yarn of all his tales.

GARCÍA: (*aside*) What dread unhappiness indeed were mi‹
if that the tale the king told unto her were one of lov‹
But, no, that cannot be, so closely following upon his honor‹
He will not play me such a turn of ill for all the loyalty ‹
late have shown. Doubtless he does not care to enter no‹
to dine with his servants at the selfsame board. I shall rep‹
to him in such a mode that he will not perceive I know h‹
rank. (*Aloud*): Milord, pray favor me and enter now, if b‹
to take a morsel of our meal, willingly served. We ask yo‹
not for pay. The apple Adam ate was not so sweet.

# None Beneath the King

(*Enter* BRAS, *carrying something to eat, also a covered jar*)

BRAS: A gentleman begs to say you're waited for.

MENDO: Ah, Blanca, how came cruelty to you?
   (*Exit*)

BLANCA: García would have me so.

GARCÍA: Is that the tale?

BLANCA: He still persists. But trust Orgaz's daughter. She answers for herself.
   (*Exit*)

BRAS: All are at table, and I shall eat alone, in silence sweet, what I have filched from out Teresa's sight. How well a man may feast in solitude! Drink, Bras, wassail!

VOICE: (*within*) Drink down!

ANOTHER: (*within*) I, too—Your health!

KING: (*within*) Come, sirs, the sun sinks in the western wave.
   (*Enter all*)

GARCÍA: Eat well, 'tis early yet. Line well your paunches.

KING: These gentlemen would fain give hunt to birds upon the open fields.

GARCÍA: You could return and spend the night with us.

KING: That cannot be.

GARCÍA: I give you each a bed of purest white, and pillows decked with fairest country flowers, and Holland's newest sheets.

KING: Your word were law, García, but we cannot bide our time. Our weekly service to our royal chief begins tomorrow, and we all must be at court. Blanca, farewell; farewell, García.

GARCÍA: May Heaven attend you.

KING: On some other day we shall converse with much more time to spare.
   (*Exeunt* KING *and* HUNTSMEN)

MENDO: Fair countrywoman, witness my distress, and think of me at times.

BLANCA: I tell you, sir, that story must be settled with my husband.

GARCÍA: What said you then?

MENDO: May Heaven send you both a long and happy life.
BLANCA: Farewell, kind sir of the tale.
MENDO: I go as one who dies. Farewell.
  (*Exit*)
GARCÍA: Farewell. And you, who are as fair as day, come to the garden, which invites my soul with promises of peace far from the voice of anxious courtiers who beg preferment —indifferent masters, favors tardy-given, erring hopes, ambition's arrogance, and those with hearts of adamant who seek to overthrow their enemies in war, or plow the main their guide the Polar star. What envy must they feel who left from here today, and make their road back to the court. Ah, by your heavenly eyes, dear Blanca mine, this is the first sad day that ever came into my peaceful life.
BLANCA: What ails you, love?
GARCÍA: The tale the courtier told.
BLANCA: Come, dear companion, let's to the garden. That's an idle tale.

# ACT II

(SCENE I. *The Court*)

QUEEN: Your strange account has much affected me; I promise you to do my uttermost to win their pardon. For his royal highness has lauded Blanca and García so, that I admire the beauty of the one and marvel at the valor of the other. Such circumstances led to their sweet union that it would seem the children, as their sires, were brought to birth beneath the selfsame star.

COUNT: The count's part in the said conspiracy lacks proper proof. Don Sancho of La Cerda, leaving his prison, fled with his small Blanca, who then was but a fledgling two years old. At that time I commanded the frontier against Aragon, and thither Cerda thought to trace his way, his daughter in his arms. But soon, exhausted by the journey's length, so grievously did he begin to ail (lodged in a wayside hamlet), that despite my tenderest aid he lived but two days more. In silent grief I gave him sepulture, and overcome with pity for the child, despatched a soldier with the hapless babe to old Orgaz. A laborer brought her up, until one day they gave her to García, whom I had chosen and whom she held dearly. Heaven had planned their union in the skies, that they might mingle their parental boons.

QUEEN: I promise you, I shall effect their pardon.

(*Enter* BRAS)

BRAS: Egad! I've glided everywhere around, and searched as diligently as a monk. I've founded him without shouting, too. Milord, I kiss your hands and feet.

COUNT: You're welcome, Bras.

QUEEN: Who is this man?
COUNT: A servant of García's.
QUEEN: Let him step forward.
BRAS: Ah! What heavenly looks! What eyes! Milady, if *you* b
 the countess, you have no flattering fortune in your mate
COUNT: What news from yonder, my good fellow?
BRAS: Well, no couriers run from Milan to our place, so tha
 I really have no news to tell. Now what's the noise of wa
 that fills this court?
COUNT: I am engaged in raising all the funds.
BRAS: Most willingly I give my little mite that peace may reig
 where *I* live. I do swear, I feel a good deal more at eas
 asleep, than camping back of ramparts out in Flanders,
 in a cart at Mancha.
QUEEN (*regarding a letter in her hand*): He writes well.—
 solemn style, and an incisive phrase.
COUNT: He is most learned.
QUEEN: It quite seems to me one needs must be, to find du
 praise at court.
 (*Enter* DON MENDO)
MENDO: His Highness waits for you.
QUEEN: Your sash of red becomes you well.
MENDO: It is because of you His royal Majesty has honore
 me.
COUNT: I, too, may claim a share in the event.
MENDO: Yours was the presentation, mine the asking.—Your
 was the information.—Yesterday, as we together fared t
 Castañar, he gave this ensign to me, worthy Count. (*Aside
 I went there free, but I returned a slave!
 (*Enter* TELLO)
TELLO: (*to the* COUNT) His Highness calls.
COUNT: I go.—Wait, Bras, for me.
BRAS: Hold. Read this little note.
COUNT: (*to* MENDO) Pray entertain this gentleman until
 shall return.
BRAS: I feel so out of place. Despatch me hence. The palac
 and its stifling-sweet perfumes were made for lords, not fo
 a country gawk.

## None Beneath the King

COUNT: A moment——
  (*Exeunt* COUNT *and* TELLO)
MENDO: I must know this servant better.
BRAS: I wonder if I may address this man. I say, how pleased you our fair Castañar on yesterafternoon, Milord?
MENDO: (*aside*) O, God of love, a thousand times upon your altar, I'll pledge burnt offerings. In this menial you send me remedy for all my ills. Ah, Blanca, how I suffer for love of thee! What agony! Would that I had never beheld fair Castañar! Would that my sorry eyes had never seen thee! Would to God that before Alphonso had ventured to thy land a scimitar had cut me dead in war. Ah, would to Heaven, fair peasant, that I might be slave unto the cruel, beauteous asp which thou servest, and which causes all my grief! How gladly would I forfeit wealth and rank to see my Blanca for a single day, and were it but to herd her rambling flock!
BRAS: The deuce, Milord! What ails you? Here you jump and bound and dart around in all directions! Why, surely a tarantula has stung you, or else you are in love.
MENDO: (*aside*) Love, be my guide. From this man must I learn if I may see fair Blanca. (*aloud*) Tell me, fellow, what's your name?
BRAS: My name? It's Bras.
MENDO: And tell me whence you hail.
BRAS: From Ajefrín, and at your service, sir.
MENDO: Of noble stock?
BRAS: The Brases\* of Castile.
MENDO: I know as much.
BRAS: Quite true. I'm ancient stock. Although I boast no wealth, I trace my line back to a song of the Nativity.
MENDO: You're finely built.
BRAS: Remarkably, in fact, just see that perfect foot—and thump this chest, as husky as a medlar tree. And say, just view these sloe black eyes.
MENDO: And tell me, Bras, you've got good wits?

---
\*Which is as "noble," say, as the name Smith or Jones.

Bras: Well, I should say I had; for any sorry chap knows more than I.

Mendo: What would you say to serving me at court? The pay is high.

Bras: Kind sir, I may want wit, but really, there's no need of parleying, and if you wish to broach some charge to me, why, bring it forth.

Mendo: Good, Bras. Here, take this purse.

Bras: Upon my oath, this fellow jests with me. Well, then, give me your hand.

Mendo: And gold crowns, too.

Bras: I quite believe so. Yet, to spare deceit, I'll see if it be empty. Right you are. 'Tis money, and from that I may infer a corresponding favor on my part. Good words pay well.

Mendo: Yes. Merely that you tell how I may best contrive to see your mistress.

Bras: For evil or for good?

Mendo: To say to her I suffer, and adore her passionately.

Bras: So may you live, I deeply feel for you. Beneath this coat I hide a tender breast; though rough I be, soft love has pierced me through, until my heart's a veritable sieve. Now I can plan an advantageous scheme. These nights García spends a-hunting boars, while she, in dress, awaits his late return, alone and unprotected. Now if you should enter by a balcony, you'd find her, half asleep. Till dawn she bides his coming. This happens oft to him who leaves at home a lady fair to go upon the hunt.

Mendo: You trifle with me?

Bras: Nay, the matter's so. Betimes I'm wont to enter late at night, over the balconies, thus to prevent my knocking at the door; or else, perhaps, Teresa will not open for me. Then I grope around like any stumbling goat to find the sling which old Belardo's left behind the grating. And I find her there, still watching silently for her García. And thus she scans the stars until the day, musing upon her arm.

Mendo: I vow, in you love sends me promise of a quick relief.

Bras: Then take you my advice.

Mendo: And you, more money....

RAS: This is not pandering.

MENDO: Upon my soul, Blanca, this night shall make thee known to me. He who would reach the sun must scale the clouds.

(*Exit* MENDO. *Enter the* KING *and* COUNT)

KING: Such is the man. I know you will approve my raising him aloft to highest rank, and crowning him with full nobility.

COUNT: He is discreet and valiant. Without doubt, there shine in him the virtues requisite to make him captain And I truly know that what experience has failed to give, his prudence and his valor will supply.

KING: Your praise will gain him favor from my men. They know full well that it is law to you never to speak unto their royal chief unless real merit crowns your applicant. Bring him tomorrow, then, my worthy count.

(*Exit* KING)

COUNT: (*to* BRAS) I know that even though it grieve you much you show the blood you spring from, when there's need.

BRAS: Command me, then, for I expect no more.

COUNT: Then, Bras, be off, and let García know: the money that he sent has been received. At present that is all, for very soon I'll see him, or reply some other day.

BRAS: Truth, 'tis not much to carry off with me! What useless, long delay! Just like the court. Much labor, and withal, but little fruit.

(SCENE II. *Woods*)

(GARCÍA *in hunting guise, armed with knife and musket*)

GARCÍA: Wide, leafy woods of mine, so bright at day, how dark you are when Morpheus bathes the night in Lethean waters, till that Tithon's spouse full proudly plumed and crowned with the rose surveys in you the skill where mars excels, panting with eager breath in hot dispute; for fury guides the chase—war's substitue. I am the living scourge of all you beasts, who train myself, a noble blood, to be the fame of Castañar in Algeciras, nourished within your grottoes, over your fields, a Spanish Hercules of all this range. To tyrants every finger of my hand is as a nail. This land is unto me a hive of wax, and prodigal in meat. 'Tis I alone avenge the deprecations of wolf and bear alike. My thriving goats and simple sheep need fear no mountain pirate. And when he falls upon the timid flock, straightway I rush into the bloody fray; my dogs, an idle audience, gaze on. My shepherds trust the valor of my arm, and sleep at ease upon their grassy beds, until the morning sun bids them arise to greet the day with torpid, weary limbs. Thus stand I sentinel over all the herd, and when I've held at bay the mountain thief, my shepherds tread amidst the spoils I've wrought, where wolves lie thicker than the blades of grass. What copious hive, distilling in its cells that sweet and limpid liquor, merits more a staunch defense against the prowling bear? For this alone, thanks to the speeding lead, the bees amidst these sunny, smiling fields possess one enemy the less. 'Twas sunset, and he had robbed two hives, transporting them unto a fountain brimmed with crystal rays, to drown the busy bees amidst their work, the better to enjoy their honeyed flood. I followed after, and he left the fount with troubled waters, colored by his blood. This night a boar approached that rivulet, to slake his thirst within its crystal beverage, his lamp the light that Phoebus lends to Cynthia. I viewed him, face to face; he stood his ground, measuring his pace, and with his ivory tusks, which gleamed like knives of steel, he beat the path. A bullet, swift as thought, sped to his head. And straight the echo filled the vale around with sounds of powder and the beast's last groans. Now both shall hang as trophies over my door, though ugly be they. And my Blanca fair shall plant her heel upon their conquered napes, and for a grace so happy, all shall say that even after death a corpse may taste true gladness, and that even 'midst the worst of fates, a brute may yet aspire to joy. But hark! That sound was uttered by a boar.—He starts, and makes precipitous return; his sharpened sense has heard some distant sound, for, so far off, he still has heard the charge of bullets in the arquebuse, and felt my hand arranging them upon the hill. For when the bristling boar but gets the sound of whistling lead, or scents the quivering bow, he flees the threatening noise on wings of fear.

(*Enter* DON MENDO, *followed by a valet with a ladder of rope*)

MENDO: For this, O tyrant Love, from great Toledo hast thou enticed me to the mountains' home—to lose myself among confusing briers? Yet what was I to await, I, blinded one, who did but choose a blind one for a guide? But I have brought a ladder, thus to climb, O Blanca, to the heights of your abode. And I would undertake the selfsame deed, even wert thou not the daughter of these hills,—of lowly birth with no protecting husband. Even wert thou goddess in a thunderous sphere, or wert thou, beauteous Blanca, a heavenly star, just as I seek thee in this lowly place, so would I rise unto the firmament and do the very deed I now attempt. Even though earth should crumble unto dust, and heaven itself dissolve in stifling fumes.

GARCÍA: The valiant beast already heard the stir these people made before it reached my ears.

MENDO: 'Neath this October moon the hunter's wont to chase the boar. I'll call. Halloo—Halloo!

VALET: Halloo—Halloo!

GARCÍA: Confound them! Why these cries? Why call you thus?

MENDO: Is Castañar far off?

GARCÍA: Two paces, and you're there.

MENDO: We've lost our way.

GARCÍA: This rivulet runs parallel to the road.

MENDO: What time is it?

GARCÍA: It lacks a bit to two.

MENDO: Whence come you?

GARCÍA: Straight from Hades. Go your way, and trouble not my hunting. Otherwise, I should get angry.

MENDO: And when shines the moon?

GARCÍA: Until it sets.

MENDO: See how the peasant is, amidst his fields.
GARCÍA: Just like a noble at court.
MENDO: And is there no mistake?
GARCÍA: 'Tis as I say.
MENDO: You're formidable.
GARCÍA: Sir, you do not know what crime it is thus to intrude on me.
MENDO: And who are you?
GARCÍA: García of Castañar. The mountain's scourge, who never denies his name.
MENDO: (*aside*) O Love, thou hast compassion—hold him back, and let him not impede my tense desires, nor let my hope miscarry in his house. And that I may behold fair Blanca's form, lend me thy wing the sooner to arrive. García, good night to you.
GARCÍA: I bid the same. I've lost my opportunity to hunt—'tis irretrievable tonight. To house I shall return across the mountain path. And since 'tis so, lend ear, you cave-born beasts; come forth, descend you o'er the valley's slope, and dwell this night in peace. Your greatest foe goes off to home to seek a calm repose, not on hard rocks, but in a downy bed. And having thrust my arquebus aside, my manner change within my spouse's arms. Night's Argus, Polyphemus of the day, shall see my actions tender, or at war, for in this breast there lie encased two hearts, the one of wax, the other hardest bronze; the wax for home, the bronze to rule the mount.

(SCENE III. *Room at Castañar*)

(DOÑA BLANCA; TERESA *with a candle, which she places on a buffet*)

BLANCA: Speed on, cold night, and let Aurora bring García from the fields, where hunts he now, back to rest. Come quickly, light and day, and let the heavens flood the field with rays, let the sungod's chariot rise, that he may see in sending me his beams, the first of lovers to watch for day, and to abhor the night.

TERESA: 'Twere better that you waited thus a-bed, your arms at rest on whitest, softest sheets. For by my very credo, I do vow that even were Bras (who lingers still at court) my husband, I should wait for him with snores.

BLANCA: My duties call for more.

TERESA: Nay, let me add, I'd buffet him not gently, should he come and wake me with the noise of his return. But since you *will* await your lord's arrival, pray sit you down. I'll fetch Belardo here, who will beguile your waiting.— But he comes.

(*Enter* BELARDO)

BELARDO: What! Do I see the sun shining at night? Then Castañar is the antipodes of Spain.

BLANCA: Belardo, seat yourself.

BELARDO: And you,—to bed.

BLANCA: To sleep in such a calm would be to miss Aurora.

BELARDO: Whom do you await?

BLANCA: My soul.

BELARDO: What folly his to wander forth till dawn, and leave you waiting here until the morn.

BRAS: (*within*) Yes, I come from Toledo,
    Fair Teresa;
    Yes, I come from Toledo,
    Not from France.

TERESA: Here comes my gallant!

BELARDO: I shall show him in.

TERESA: Now by your leave I'll to the balcony, and ask him pertly what he's brought for me.

BRAS: And if the basilisk be good, Calibaza's cross is better.

TERESA: (*opening the balcony window*) Well, Bras, how do you come?

BRAS: Oh, on my feet!

TERESA: And what is it you bring me as a pledge?

BRAS: Just listen, and I'll put it into song:
    I bring you from Toledo,
    To serve you in your pleasure,

A gallant spark, Teresa,
As green as any nut.

TERESA: The devil take your verses! Where's some corset,—at least that, or some costly string of pearls?

BLANCA: What brings he? Ah—a princely gift indeed—a nut green lover that's quite savory.

(*Enter* BRAS)

BRAS: Teresa, what's amiss? I vow I die! And you embrace me not?

TERESA: Indeed I do! For all the precious presents you have brought!

BRAS: What demons women are! Whom love you most?

TERESA: My Bras.

BRAS: Then if I bring what you most love, what more could you desire?

BLANCA: Teresa, he's right. Now seat yourself, and tell us what you've seen.

BRAS: I saw a swarm of houses, and at large, a host of unemployed. In all the streets both good and bad, were heaps of hoarded filth. I saw the sky as through a narrow tube*—the people's happy faces hide disdain; summer brings eggplant;—autumn's crop is gnats.

BLANCA: No further news at court?

BRAS: Now can I see, your mischievous spirit seeks more satire. No, my plume's not of the court. With other things divert yourself until the break of day. As for the absent one, God keep him safe.

BLANCA: List, now: to him who guesses first this riddle, among you three, I'll give a costly cloth:—that one of scarlet which I made last year. First, then, Teresa,—Who is the motherless bird that cannot see her father or her son—he who was born from a dead father's seed?

TERESA: And had it gaiters and a hooded cloak?

BLANCA: The matter's plain; now give your answers, all.

TERESA: The cuckoo.

BRAS: No, the owl.

BELARDO: There is no bird to whom the case applies except

*i.e., the streets were very narrow, with projecting upper stories.

the phœnix. Nor can it be another. It alone, arises from the ashes of its father.

BLANCA: Belardo wins.

BELARDO: Hurrah! The prize is mine!

BRAS: And I have lost,—as at every other time.

BLANCA: No, I shall give you what you have deserved.

BRAS: And here's a small cap for the one who'll tell what is the dearest vice in all the world.

BLANCA: 'Tis gaming, I assert.

BRAS: Not so—that's clear.

TERESA: I say the costliest vice is that of women.

BELARDO: And I affirm the costliest pleasure of all is hunting. And I can support my claim by quoting poor Actæon's direful fate.

BRAS: Nay, wrong all three. There is no room for doubt but that the dearest vice is drunkenness, nor can another be compared with that. For though he drown a fortune in his cups, there is no way a chap retrieves his loss.

(GARCÍA *whistles within*)

BLANCA: God grant no mishap brings him thus to me!

GARCÍA: (*within*) Greetings, my faithful folk.

BRAS: Good master, welcome.

(GARCÍA *enters, and places his musket on the buffet.* BLANCA *goes to him*)

GARCÍA: How fared things in Toledo with you, Bras?

BRAS: I gave your paper to the count. He said he would reply.

GARCÍA: 'Tis well. And you, dear wife, are still awake. What did you wait, my dear?

BLANCA: I watched for day, and lingered as the goddess—the tender mother of love, awaits the hunter who leaves his nets and finds within her arms a fairer prison,—a golden chain of love, where dwells his boon. 'Tis she who shares with him her very soul, even as she shares her couch. But I, with better right, make of my arms a loving net, and to secure your fall (Oh huntsman who exceeds them all by far!) I'll trap you with the faith of turtledoves, that you may well excuse my amorous plaint. No snarling boar I consecrate to you, but in its place a bird that weeps its mate. Ah, yield

unto the tugging of love's chain and you shall hear within
its feathery realm love's gentle billing, not the mountain's
roar. I should complain that you do thus desert me, leaving my arms, to hunt at midnight hour; yet so do I adore
you, that despite those just complaints and all my tender
losses, when you return—as even now you've come—so
great my joy swells merely at your sight,—I thank you for
the qualms your absence caused.

GARCÍA: Ah, fairest Blanca, burgeoned branch of May, beside
your blooming cheek the Guadarrama is black as Ethiopia—
the sun becomes obscure,—the crystal's purity is charred to
slate. In you all beauty's power has crowned itself in lofty
consummation. And when necessity bids me go forth and
you are left complaining,—you can feel no greater grief
than I, away from you. When I return, repenting to have
gone, in vain your breast can murmur its reproach,—you
could not punish me at such glad meeting. Our souls receive alike love's joys and pains, and we are one to arrows
and to bonds. Nor vine and leafy elm are closer twined
than I to you, my Blanca. Come, my love, there is not
greater joy than to entreat with those who kindle our desire.
And though I bring you not from out night's borrowed light
the bristly boar felled by my arquebus, nor even the
poaching bear,—him that I saw descend upon the orchard,
making off with two large realms of honey, and who then,
to suit his humor, bathed his snout and hide,—instead of
trophies such as this I bring, both beautiful, and yet exceeding ugly, my captive soul, and many sweet desires, to serve
as carpet where your foot may tread. And when I ponder
on your precious worth, how small indeed my offering
seems to grow, even as small as that which I have brought.

BRAS: Sure as I live—that is Teresa there!

TERESA: And who goes there? Whose voice is that I hear?

BRAS: Satan's. Until the curate sings us both our benediction.
For a married man may find salvation in the very deed
which would, in bachelors, be esteemed a crime.

TERESA: Explain!

BRAS: By loving his wife, and multiplying.
TERESA: That's working in the vineyard of the Lord.
BLANCA: Take off the hunter's garb. I've here for you, my cherished mate, a garment sewed by me, whose odor's sweeter than the rosemary. And I can well maintain it is more fine than any Holland sheet which you could find. For when a sheet is clean, it has no need of April flowers' perfume. Come.—You, too.
(*To the servants. Exit* BLANCA)
BRAS: I've always heard it said—a woman's love is mirrored in the clothes her husband wears.
TERESA: And it has always been a proverb here that he lacks honor, and is void of love, who goes to court and brings his dame no jewels. (*Exeunt both*)
GARCÍA: The richest and most coveted of men must envy me my home of sweet delights, where truth and happiness beget such joy. The very gods must marvel at my fate. For when fair Blanca greets my lover's eyes, her very beauty satisfies desire.—Merciful Heaven! What is it greets my sight?
(DON MENDO *is seen entering furtively by the balcony. He beholds* GARCÍA *and promptly covers his face with his cloak*)
MENDO: Good God! This is García of Castañar! Take courage, heart,—the deed's beyond recall. And he who puts his trust in peasant hands can scarce expect a better fate.
GARCÍA: Sir noble, if he who stoops so low may thus be named,—if some necessity has driven you to robbery, then tell me what you wish,—for by my word, I promise you shall leave well satisfied with what my hand shall give.
MENDO: Let me return, García.
GARCÍA: That will I not, until you first discover who you are,—nor shall I brook delay—if you resist, this musket speeds a bullet to your breast.
MENDO: Take care,—make no mistake concerning me. This exigency makes us equals. Yet, if you surpass me in your reasoning, still am I first in station and in birth. (*Aside*) I

know Orgaz has told it secretly, in speaking of me. Let this sash of red across my breast bear witness who I am.

(*Throws aside his cloak, and* García *drops his musket*)

García: (*aside*) It is the king! Good God! He knows full well that I too know him.—Honor, loyalty, what shall I do? What honor counsels me, allegiance to the king in turn forbids.

Mendo: How like a peasant! He is plainly awed through fear of me or of my noble birth. Although,—to meet a humble man in fight my strength alone were matched unto the work. To think Orgaz had praised his bravery so! Well, after all, he's old. (*Aloud*) I cannot flee, nor can deny.—You have me in your home. But I assure you,—if I enter thus—

García: It was to rob me of my precious honor. How well you pay the hospitality which I and Blanca freely gave to you! See what a difference shines in both our acts. How I, offended, venerate you still, while you reward my loyalty with insult.

Mendo: (*aside*) There is no trusting an offended boor. And while I may, I'll guard myself with this. (*He seizes the musket*)

García: What are you doing? Put that weapon down,—and if I take it away from you, it is because you must know that it shall not affect this matter's end. It is enough I see your sash of red, surrounded by the sun of great Castile, which blinds my eyes.

Mendo: You recognize me, then?

García: Judge if I do.

Mendo: A person of my rank can give no satisfaction. What to do?

García: Be gone—pray God to curb your wild desires—come here no more—for I cannot average your desperate follies. —That I leave to Heaven.

Mendo: You shall be paid, García.

García: I ask you nothing.

Mendo: Let not Orgaz know this.

García: I promise it.

Mendo: Then God be with you.

## None Beneath the King

García: May He guard you well—and me and Blanca, too, from your attempts.

Mendo: Your wife——

García: Sir Noble, mention not that name! The fault is yours —I know my mate too well.

Mendo: (*aside*) Blanca, I die for you. Contrary fate! Him I offended bears me yet respect: she I adore has wounded me to death!

García: Where go you?

Mendo: To the door.

García: How blind you are—this is the way.

Mendo: You know me?

García: Pray, believe, did I not know you, your descent would be a trifle more precipitous. But here, take you this arquebus, and have good care; for robbers lurk around the mountains here, and they might do you ill, even as might I, did they not recognize you. Quick, go down, I do not wish my Blanca to learn of this.

Mendo: I must obey.

García: Make haste, no words, I say. This is no time to bandy compliments. And see that as you go you do not fall,—I would not have you stumble in my house, the sooner to despatch you hence.

Mendo: I die. (*Exit*)

García: Securely, no: I hold the ladder tight.—Fortune, a moment's fixity has tired thee! O, what a sudden change upon this sea!—How swift the winds have veered. In what a day, so happy and serene, a clear sky shoots dark thunderbolts against my peacefulness. My griefs are certain: I can trust my eyes. Alphonso, incognito, covets my wife. Unhappy me, born with the rank of Count, and cast among these hills, a courtly toiler,—to what low depths am I reduced this day! Is this the king's reward for all my service? But that shall be my sorrow,—not his blame. Silence, my aching heart, and let us seek an efficacious remedy. Such pangs, such risks are for a valiant soul. Let us make off to foreign parts with Blanca; there shall a refuge be for innocence and honor.—No! They'll say I was afraid. But then,

I need assign no cause. Simply, I am too weak to go to Algeciras: 'Tis true.—'Twere better that I tell the king of my noble birth.—But no, García, no—he then would kill you to advance his purpose. If Blanca be the cause, and if the king cannot resist, what is there to be done? Kings' passions lend no ear to reason's voice. One other course remains.—Blanca must die! (*Draws his dagger*) And with her, all dishonor. Choose, my heart, the least of evils. If not jealousy, my honor has condemned you unto death. Your life must ransom me from infamy. Forgive me, Blanca, you are free from fault,— reasons of state alone call for your death. But is it right that Honor thus should choke the voice of Justice? Aye, for providence and reason (may) see pictured future ills upon the glass of present happenings. Ah, Blanca, must I be so barbarous, so cruel—and stain your breast of jessamine with bloody flowers? No, this cannot be! Beautiful Blanca, never can my hand destroy the very mirror of my soul. But no—I laud her beauty, and forget that honor is the theme of this sad song. Let Blanca die: I soon shall follow. Courage, let one blow kill the two—a single blow transfix two breasts and liberate two souls.—A single thrust yoke our two necks in blood. This shall I do, if courage stays me true, and if, when that I raise my hand to strike, between the voice and everlasting silence, my blood freeze not within my very veins, and if the knife rebel not against its deed.

# ACT III

(SCENE I. *A Forest*)

(*Enter the* COUNT, *his horses, and* TELLO)

COUNT: Here, Tello, lead the horses by the rein. I wish to see the fragrant day afoot,—far from this mountain fast approaching morn gilds the horizon. What a charming field! And happy will you die who dwell there now, above the wranglings of philosophy. There, too, your prudent wife, whose name is white, is white in virtue, too, of Cerda's line. But if my sight be true, behind that hedge there sallies forth a heavenly looking woman, dishevelled—in distress. Without a doubt she must be beautiful: her grief is proof. (*Enter* DOÑA BLANCA, *with some of her raiment in her arms*)

BLANCA: Where do I flee, in breathless agony, in aimless haste, without protecting hand, through this deep thicket? Weep, O weep, mine eyes, and as I dress, tongues of my hapless heart, repeat unto my unresisting ears: "O tender gifts, how God ordains your fate!"

COUNT: Some sorrow stalks afoot. She seems to dress.—— She is perturbed, and wanders all alone. 'Tis not beneath a Spaniard's blood to aid in such a plight as this.

BLANCA: A man approaches.

COUNT: How fair she is!

BLANCA: I'll hide behind this bush.

COUNT: Hold, woman, bide your time.—Have you come out as did Diana, from the sparkling fount, coldly to smite the hunter bold with love, even as the beast?

BLANCA: O, twice unhappy fate,—it is the count!

COUNT: Blanca! Where go you thus?

BLANCA: I flee my husband and his murderous hand. Those

dulcet sounds upon the balcony with which the birds and
lulled me to sleep,—those were not wedding hymns the
sang in turn; no, no, O Count, they were ill-omened bird
whose song portended impious augury,—who, all day lon
and through the horrid night, instead of bridal hymns cha
threnodies. Fortune has left me. Listen to the cause—the
hasten to my house where lies there, dead, my husband.——
Dead, O Count. 'Twas but this night, my love awaited hi
within my bed, the goal of all desire, the sacred aim, th
shrine of Hymen. I invoked him there, while all the hous
lay shrouded in calm sleep. I saw him enter with the sterne
mien, brandishing over my head a knife of steel. I left m
place as one who jumps from flame,—I sought my cloth
and in bewilderment seized first this jewelled gown. Se
what a wealth of sparkling gems it bears. In haste I donne
my under-skirt, and scarcely could I find its opening, or th
girdle round its waist. Such as it was I flung it over my head
and as I did, I found a breath to think. "What does th
mean?" I begged him. To my sight he stood there as i
death. To my request came in reply a deeply heaving sigh
while from his breast and from his softened eyes streame
forth such mingled pity and such anger, I doubted whethe
this were love or ire. Then leaving me, he tenderly return
and then again he glows to heated wrath and comes to m
half like a raging beast and half a tender lover. "Blanc
mine, this instant do you die, and I fast follow." He lifts hi
arm—I wait the final blow—his voice dies in his throat—h
drops to the ground, as does the mountain rock blown by th
storm, rolling down the slopes in steep descent, falling a
last inert and mute as death. I watch his lips, his eyes, an
palest flowers usurp the spot where reddest blossom
bloomed. I seek warmth in his breath, but all in vain. An
thus he lay, hanging 'twixt life and death, until his breas
began again to throb, and he was murmuring, "Fly, un
happy Blanca, fortune keeps no scale for good or ill, and
naught can be so vile as to submit to her caprice." And
obeyed his words. I left my home, my spouse, and turne
from all, thus gathering in disorder all my clothes; running

as blind, I bled at every step and turned again to look upon my mate. O Count, let me postpone to other times the words he uttered, threatening me with death, the plaints,—the cries—the tender-harsh affronts,—advances and retreats,—dispute and doubt,—love matched with hate,—his vacillating arm, now raised in menace, dropping in remorse. I tried to soothe his fury by my tears, and sought to stay his dagger with my hand,—he yielded easily to my attempts, even as a lover who denies, when asked, that which, indeed, he freely means to give. My breast was bared to meet the cruel thrust, dissolved in tears. You should have viewed that world,—its fiery origin,—its icy end. You should have seen my terror, then, alone, aimless, in fright, and rooted to the ground. My hands grew numb,—my reason set at bay. I left him there, as leaves a fallen oak he whom the trumpet calls back to his guard, abandoning the trunk unto his foe.—How with uncertain foot I sought the keys, and failed to find the locks, veiled in the gloom! (My breath comes hard)—I scratched at every hinge,—and O, the agonies that wracked my soul! I crossed the threshold—wandered to the thicket, whose spreading branches tore my flowing hair.—O would to God my tresses then had hanged me! See to it, Count, and help my ailing soul. I pardon all,—it is not possible his arm could menace me without just cause. His very act is its own punishment, as is my anguish discipline to me. There lies he in a swoon, perhaps now dead. O valorous Count, you of a noble race, whose forehead bears a lustrous diadem,—so may the silvery beard that sweeps your breast exterminate all traces of the Moors, as quickly as you rush unto his aid. If that he really live, God soothe his rage;—the wheel of Fortune turns once more to us: be you our arbiter, for pitying fate has sent you as the cure of all our ills. Grant favor, staunch protection,—counsel us,—for lo, my eyes behold no thieving throng, but see, illustrious Count, your honored self, the glory of Illan, Toledo's boast. Upon the road to death have I found life.

COUNT: This matter calls for prudence. Tello, hear me: Blanca, you may rely upon my judgment. (TELLO *approaches*) Take

then this horse, who ever serves me well, and without
further parley or excuse fare to Toledo under Tello's guide;
this is the first of all things to be done. Go to the court:
appear before the queen,—meanwhile, I burn to hasten to
your home, for it shall ever be my first concern to serve you,
Blanca, and to shield you well.

TELLO: Come then, sad mistress.

BLANCA: How I fain would see García first.

COUNT: 'Twere better as I say.

BLANCA: Your word shall be my law. Come, let us go.

(SCENE II. *García's Home*)

(*Enter* GARCÍA, *with an unsheathed dagger in his hand*)

GARCÍA: Blind homicide, O whither do I go? Honor, where
takest me, without my heart, without the very essence of my
life? Farewell, O moiety of my soul. My sun, whom some
dark cloud has plunged into eclipse. No, no: if that my
spouse were truly dead, day had not light, nor I a life. She
dead! It is not so, for Heaven grants her breath,—her husband slew her, but her lover yet desires her. I would see her
even now—her room is empty, and the door is wide, and
here the dagger in my clutch, unstained. And see: I live—
then she can not be dead. Blanca alive? And I, woe's me
sans honor? Blind lover that I am, and cowardly spouse. I
saw the king within my very home, seeking my treasure
there, and through a noble, the law laid down my course,
and clemency was due the king—to Blanca, tyranny. How
many times the tyrant steel was raised, how many times my
heart restrained the thrust! If she be dead, 'tis just she so
should die; if that she live, her death must pay the breach.
Blanca, my Blanca, what am I to do? But what can you
reply?—For there is left but death to choose.

(*Enter the* COUNT)

COUNT: I beg your grace to tell against what Moorish scimitar
tonight you've raised that dagger in your coward's hand!
Against a feeble woman, knowing not that she is more than

peasant? Pray recall, when you proposed to marry her, I said you were her equal. There I lied, because her ancestor was of La Cerda's line; her noble father was a count. Nay more, and were she but the peasant which you thought, is there a cause for shame when you behold the king come here to visit, making you a captain in this war, at my request? He sends me emissary, forth to you, to take you to Toledo back with me. And this is your repayment? You kill her who is the very sight within mine eyes? By Heaven, this fool who speaks to you will shed for but a drop of that fair woman's blood, full every drop of life blood in his veins!

GARCÍA: Who is she—Blanca?

COUNT: She's your wife—enough.

GARCÍA: Be calm: who said I wished to slay my wife?

COUNT: An angel whom I found upon the mount, who, midst the thicket, wept her pearly tears into the running brooks, and fanned the air with sorry sighs.

GARCÍA: And Blanca, where is *she*?

COUNT: I sent her, with a servant, to the court. There will she move within her proper sphere.

GARCÍA: Now may you slay me, Lord! O, give me death! Blanca at court. Can I survive that news? O insult, honor, grief, how now withstand the mingled fury of your fell assault? My wife is at the palace, Count? The king, whom Heaven guard, sends me as captain off, heading his ranks away to Algeciras? And I a peasant in his real belief! Please God he do not sully with affronts these honors which he grants. Oh! Would to Him the woman whom you bred at old Orgaz's but for my death, were but a lowly peasant, and were not beautiful. Oh, would to Him, before she had inflamed my ardent breast, this dagger had but cleft my heart in twain. Then, too, would you be spared the venger's task, the killing me—for I should first have died. What sweet decease that were,—no more to hear that she is where a mighty power attacks and I cannot defend her. Know, then, Count, she is a beauteous vessel, rich in cargo,—a pirate seeks her as she sails the sea—she rides at harbor in his treacherous port. First did he chase her in her own.—She

lacked protection,—helmsman none, without a mast. I well
may fear that she be overcome through force or stratagem
by him who seeks! I could not bring myself to strike her
down, even as was right. Believe me, there was cause, although that must be passed in silence, Count, remember
that a fool in his own home knows more than a wise man
in another's.

COUNT: You know me?

GARCÍA: From Toledo are you come, in lineage from Illan.

COUNT: Respect is due me?

GARCÍA: Aye. I have always held you as a father.

COUNT: Am I your friend?

GARCÍA: Yes, that is clear enough.

COUNT: For what are you beholden unto me?

GARCÍA: Favors a-plenty.

COUNT: Do I value truth?

GARCÍA: Most highly.

COUNT: And my valor?

GARCÍA: Great, indeed.

COUNT: You know that I am ruler of a realm?

GARCÍA: With universal approbation—aye.

COUNT: Then you may well rely upon my counsel, who are so
saddened and afflicted. Sir, tell me your grief as son to father
would. Recount me all your ills, your tribulation, nor fear
you Blanca. Noble though she be, she is but woman.

GARCÍA: I could kill you, Count, if you should dare affirm that
even the sun or yet bright gold, both in their purest lustre,
were fit comparison to her fair name.

COUNT: Although you speak as should a husband, yet your
sad restraint does not allay my doubts. Have done—we are
alone—by this sword's cross I must give succor and protect
her well, even as a daughter; for, in such a case, gladly I'd
banish pity, even love, to save her honor. Tell—is it
jealousy?

GARCÍA: Of nobody.

COUNT: What ails you, then?

GARCÍA: Such grief as is beyond the power of your cure.

# None Beneath the King

COUNT: What can we, then, in such a pressing case?
GARCÍA: Does not the king command you to escort me? On to Toledo, then. His majesty knows who I am?
COUNT: His majesty knows not.
GARCÍA: On to Toledo, Count.
COUNT: Come then, García.
GARCÍA: Lead you the way.
COUNT: (*aside*) Your honor and your life are threatened, Blanca, for such quiet bodes a dangerous thought. His lips are sealed in silence.
GARCÍA: Blanca, are you not at court? Are you not gone, did you not leave me? Then what once would be clear foresight now becomes a just revenge.

(SCENE III. *At Court*)

(*Enter the* QUEEN *and* BLANCA)

QUEEN: I pledge my aid to you. Believe me, Countess, I truly grieve to listen to your woes.
BLANCA: Countess? She means not me. Your majesty, you quite forget my station.
QUEEN: Cousin mine, Blanca de La Cerda, come, embrace me.
BLANCA: Although I hear, and know you must speak truth, I still insist I am a peasant born,—so lowly that I spent my childhood days with old Orgaz, without a father's care.
QUEEN: Such a father, yours, once almost king of Castile. You are the daughter of Don Sancho, Blanca. Your husband is as noble as yourself. And since you are at ease, remain a while, until the count returns. Tell not your name, and meanwhile I shall order your reception.

(*Exit* QUEEN. *Enter* DON MENDO)

BLANCA: O Heaven, can there be one to whom harsh fate sends ills so thick apace, and boons so scarce as unto me? Can I sustain such blows? Joy gives not life to me; grief slowly kills. O, husband, in what anguish you have left me! How grief has drained my eye of all its tears, and numbed my heart. (*Puts her handkerchief to her eyes*)

MENDO: O, fairest peasant maid, who rivals April's fragrance in her mien, pray draw aside that subtle veil of tears, or you shall string the 'kerchief's hem with pearls. Who are you? I am sent here by the queen to care for you. I've waited here.

BLANCA: Have done, Sir Knight who bears the sash of red.

MENDO: Fair maid, you know me then?

BLANCA: (*aside*) I do, but such my plight, I scarcely know myself.

MENDO: Since that cruel day when I first saw thee, my adoring heart has sighed to place itself before thy feet.

BLANCA: (*aside*) This is the very summit of my woes. This only lacked.

MENDO: I sought your house last night. With wings of love I flew to gaze at you. My kind fate changed, but not my passion's faith; your husband met me, and resisted me with courtesy.

BLANCA: What's that you say?

MENDO: Blanca, the lover seeks his fortune all in vain; he finds it not, except by accident, just as I find you now.

BLANCA: Now know I, knight, that your insane desires have brought my woes. Now must I suffer and keep silent counsel.

(*Enter* GARCÍA *at first unseen by both*)

GARCÍA: Here shall I wait Orgaz. What do I see!

MENDO: I'll soothe your sadness with the balm of love.

BLANCA: Go—sooner can you hope to dim a star than you can take my honor's light away.

GARCÍA: (*aside*) O, valiant woman—O, usurping king!

MENDO: I beg you, be less cruel.

BLANCA: I have a husband.

MENDO: And I have power; my arms will suit you better than his in whose embrace no honor lies.

BLANCA: Not so—lowborn or born of highest rank, the best of gallants is of far less worth than is the worst of husbands.

GARCÍA: (*aside*) How can I, a nobleman, support such vile offense? The king believes himself unknown. I'll speak!

MENDO: And how shall you resist?

BLANCA: With firm defense.
MENDO: Who gave such rigor?
BLANCA: He who gave to Rome eternal fame.
MENDO: What vain resisting parley! Who can oppose me now?
GARCÍA: I can—yes, I! Only my woe and my relationship permit me here to match my earthborn self against your heavenly rays of majesty. I know too well what remedy were fitting, nor can I take it with security. For love has raised one wall against my rigor, and fealty has forthwith raised another.
BLANCA: García, my husband!
MENDO: (*aside*) Aid me, strategy!
GARCÍA: O, ill-starred beauty!—tyrannous perfidy!
BLANCA: My happiness was great.
GARCÍA: My sadness greater.
BLANCA: Thank me for love.
GARCÍA: Avenge my jealousy, since honor finds no cure for all my grief. This remedy alone: Come, Blanca, mine, come back to Castañar.
MENDO: She's in my power, till further orders. For I have been told 'twere for the peace of both to guard her well.
GARCÍA: Heaven thank you for your pains. It is not just that you should guard from me her whom, indeed, I rather must defend from you. No, no,—it is not meet, nor has it ever been seen that wolves should tend a flock, or bears guard hives. And to my grief, Milord, you would become, should I not take my Blanca from your care, a blind, voracious bear, a famished wolf, intent on stealth,—impelled to blackest crime.
BLANCA: Dismiss me, sir.
MENDO: Blanca, you are my ward. You shall not leave.
GARCÍA: This is not due my love.
MENDO: Still it must be.
GARCÍA: That is a sternness, sir, born of injustice.
MENDO: (*aside*) I must see the queen, and force this woman to remain at court. (*Aloud.*) You must not stray from here. I order it, who may command.
  (*Exit* MENDO)

GARCÍA: Good God, patience I beg, for valor has deserted me. Oh, fate, to save my honor means to break my faith; was ever such inclemency? Again must I recur to homicide? But no,—the soul cleft from my body, all my grief would wax immortal, for there are such woes as end not with our life.

BLANCA: García, heaven guard you; Phenix, live on eternally, while I though innocent, will gladly die for you, whose bitterness I am. And it shall be a consolation that I died through you,—live then, and I shall live within your breast.

GARCÍA: I cannot leave the place. No, he has ordered, He who must be obeyed.

BLANCA: Return, García, and if it grieve you that, our bonds untied, I died not at your hands,—I lay my life before your feet. I know now who you are. And since my death redeems your honored name, thrust in the steel with your delaying arm, and rescue honor through a sad maid's death. I wish it—welcome it from your hand. If I have feared you as a tyrant, yet, I beg you now. Last night I feared to lose you, and now I share your grief. You cannot live sans honor— let me die that you may live. All that I ask is gratitude for this.

GARCÍA: I know your innocence—in vain your speech. For who is faultless can redeem no wrong by suffering for its commission. No, your death would but accentuate my sorrow. I honorless, and you without a stain. Love cries against your death—while honor smarts to have you live. I fear love blames in vain, when honor thus absolves me. I'm at war 'twixt reason's power and fear of majesty. To slay were barbarous; vengeance is treason. Such my dilemma—such my crushing woes—they strive in rivalry to follow on.— Perplexingly they swarm about my head; I can but feel them;—succor there is none. Blanca, advise me.—But of what avail, if that the remedy must cause more pangs?

BLANCA: If I must die, García, withhold it not; there's tyranny where death is long delayed.

## None Beneath the King

GARCÍA: My cherished wife! What contrary extremes!
BLANCA: Come from here, husband.
GARCÍA: Let us first await Him who alone can keep us from our home. Stand off from me: we must dissemble, Blanca.
   (*Enter the* KING, *the* QUEEN, *the* COUNT, DON MENDO *and the royal suite*)
KING: (*to the* QUEEN) Blanca at court, you say? García, too? This so contents me, that I vow, today they both shall have from us what they deserve.
MENDO: It is not well to add this public honor to one who fears to satisfy his own. You may believe my words, Your Majesty.
KING: (*aside*) That's small good will. (*aloud*) There stand García and Blanca. Approach. I wish you both to know my love.
GARCÍA: (*still mistaking* MENDO *for the* KING) Heaven guard you, knight, first let us kiss your feet.
MENDO: (*pointing to the king*) There stands the king.
GARCÍA: (*aside*) Outraged honor!—Heaven! What foul deceit is this? (*aloud*) We both, Milord,—give us your hand.—We scarce deserve such mark—You well may see——
KING: Stand off,—release your hand.—The color is quite vanished from your face.
GARCÍA: (*aside*) Lost honor saps the blood of all well-born. (*aloud*) Now hear my secret. You are as a sun, when I bow down before your blinding rays my face reveals the consequence.
KING: You've been wronged.
GARCÍA: And know who's wronged me. That perturbs my soul.
KING: Then point him out.
GARCÍA: (*to the* KING, *then to* MENDO) That will do, Milord. Sir, I would wish a word with you outside. It is important, and the king must not look on.——
MENDO: I wait you in the anteroom.
   (*Exit* DON MENDO)
GARCÍA: Courage, my heart, take courage.
KING: Whither, García?

GARCÍA: To carry out your order,—since I see you have not been the offender.

(*Exit* GARCÍA)

KING: He is grieved at his offense. Now must I go and see whom he shall indicate.

GARCÍA: (*within*) Knight of the sash, know,—this is honor!

KING: Peasant, stay your hand!

MENDO: (*within*) This is my death!

(*Enter* GARCÍA)

GARCÍA: Alphonso, I affirm that I am not the peasant whom you think, nor do I violate the sanctity of these great royal halls without just cause. Beneath this rustic garb flows noble blood, allied to mountains but in ways and habit. You are the son of Ferdinand, whose death, though early, left the world a far famed name;—you were a year-old child at his decease. The Moors were then at camp, and off at Asia the Turks were laying plans to found their empire. And at Castile the Laras and the Cerdas were, 'midst a host of others, powerful, and, with a few, they strongly, rightly, claimed the crown you wear, which Castile gave to you. So loyal are the Spaniards to the core. And it was bruited 'round that Count Bermudo, who was full regent both in peace and war, conspired (because he wished to quell the tumult, and hush the diffidence caused by your youth) to place an older king upon the throne. And it is said proposed Don Sancho of La Cerda; I argue not the merits of this case:—be it as said or not—but those in charge, fearing lest he who scarcely was a brook should swell to Danube's size, or that the spark should flame to lightning—that this little shrub wax a robust trunk,—they seized the count and thrust him into prison at Burgos. Don Sancho fled to cover with his child,—a two-year-old girl. He feared his innocence were scarcely safe in your tribunal's hands. And lo, that cloud which long obscured your throne was quickly dissipated. Then his wife, nearby, came to the city's bounds, and brought a little son of hers, quite five years old. She begged the guards at night that they might yield to let her see her husband. Tears were vain;

a thousand crowns of gold succeeded better. "I come not, spouse," she said, "to raise thy grief, here where the executioner awaits thee. No, 'tis to end thy woes and give thee freedom." Forthwith she drew from out her golden hair a file to wrest the chains from off his limbs. Once free, she gave to him her gathered wealth, threw over him her cloak in such disguise, he passed the guards together with her son. And while he urged his Andalusian steeds, she made the bed as if a human mass lay resting there. The trick was soon discovered. They seized her, and she never left alive, but went from prison to her sepulchre. The count made his abode midst rock and crag, dwelling within the darkness of a cave, full deftly hid from the pursuing band.—His noble buskins changed to leathern clouts, his courtly silk transformed to mountain skins. One day he saw his image in a brook, which purled in crystals down its docky bend,—an uncouth savage dressed in skins of beasts, his beard and hair unkempt across his shoulder, parted at random like a clump of reeds. In vain he sought himself in the reflection. That was no man he saw—it was a beast. Till summer came, and with its heavenly brush gave the last telling sweep to earth's broad canvas. He lived on wild-fruit culled from withered branches, drank purest water and preserved sweet nuts in rudest vases. By the scanty light that strayed on past the mouth of that dark cave,—a relic of the flood of ancient days, he was his child's fond tutor. For a while, his work was vain—his eyes awoke in darkness,—a mere instructed animal. And soon, the youth left books and courted bravery, coming at night with trophies to his lair, bedecked with purple blood from tusky boars. The father's visage furrowed deep with age, when in his weakness, not decrepitude, he heard death's call, and said unto his son, "Orgaz dwells near, go fetch him fast, my son, tell him to come to this nocturnal haunt, and bring a priest; a relative, a friend sends for him quickly ere he dies." I fled without delaying for credentials then. They come, and find the count in death's last throes;—he tries to speak—the others listen, mute. "Behold,

Orgaz, a bolt dissolved in smoke,—a statue sunk to dust—Nebuchadnezzar thrust down from might." And clasping me, went on, "This is my son, and I am Count Bermudo. Let him in you and in these precious jewels find refuge. Be to him as father would." Even as he spoke, within the priestly arm, pale—and the eyes of soul and body dark—death cut the knot that bound him still to life. We carried him by night to Castañar, there to receive its plaints. The jewels of night served as our torches. There, with all my wealth I bought me lands and organized a home, and married Blanca, satisfying thus my love and the desires of the count. With envy none, I lived 'twixted plow and yoke in shelter against your ire.—Until last night I met that treacherous guest who viewed my wife with his lascivious eye. Thinking 'twas you, I stayed my vengeance with my loyalty. But once I learned his real identity, my pride of blood returned; I shook my fear, and honor cried for vengeance. Firm I grasp the shining blade—and thrust it through his heart. There—see him dead, for it were vile to let so fell a wretch live in your sight, though he be scion of nobility—Grandee of Spain, and fast in royal grace, second to you alone. Such then am I, and such my grievance. Here I stand before you a criminal. Behold my murderous arm. Lead on the executioner. As long as shall my neck remain on these strong shoulders, I will be wronged by *none beneath the king*.

QUEEN: What can you say to this?
KING: I am perturbed.
BLANCA: What matters my poor life? I am the sad ill-fated daughter of the Cerda line. And if my spouse pay forfeit with his breath, let both halves share the death as both shared life.
KING: What means this, Count?
COUNT: 'Tis true. Necessity called forth the explanation.
QUEEN: I am pledged to work in favor of their pardon.
KING: (*to* BLANCA *and* GARCÍA) Come, come to my arms, García and Blanca, both. And to your care, Count, I confide the war.

García: Then let the rolling drum give forth its call, for I, the scourge of all the Moors, advance, and seas of crimson shall o'errun their fields. Thus finish and begin my signal deeds.

## Production Notes

This anthology is designed for your reading pleasure. In most instances a performance fee is required from any group desiring to produce a play. Usually the organization that handles such performance rights also publishes individual production copies of the plays. Any group interested in additional information concerning performance fees or production copies of the plays in this anthology should apply to the following companies:

| | |
|---|---|
| THE SHEEP WELL | Charles Scribner's Sons<br>597 Fifth Avenue<br>New York 17, N.Y. |
| LIFE IS A DREAM | Houghton Mifflin Co.<br>2 Park Street<br>Boston 7, Mass. |
| NONE BENEATH THE KING | Haldeman-Julius Co.<br>Girard, Kansas |